The text pages of this book were printed with vegetable oil-based inks containing no petroleum products.

ISBN 0-9753470-0-4

Special thanks to the NPR staff, their friends, and their families for sharing stories and recipes with us. This book would not exist without the creativity and dedication of Barbara Sopato, Maggy Sterner, Jacques Couglin, Jeeun Lee, Nicole Todd, and countless others who offered perspectives and ideas along the way.

To order *NPR Cooks!* and other NPR products, call 1.888.677.3472 or visit the NPR Shop at http://shop.npr.org

Foreword

This is a cookbook put together by the same people that put together radio programs like *Morning Edition*® and *All Things Considered*®. You've cooked with these people before now — or at any rate you've cooked breakfast or dinner while carrying on a conversation with your radio. Certainly I do that all the time. I'm wandering around the kitchen, assembling a meal, talking back to the radio. But does it necessarily follow that all the people who keep you company while you cook are good cooks? Some of the same principles are involved — you want something that is balanced, offers variety, is basically good for you, and is also pleasant to consume. That could describe a radio program or a good breakfast.

In fact, we do have a lot of good cooks at NPR®. As you will see as you read through this book, most of us associate food with love and family. And we often include our colleagues in that family. Thanksgiving dinner is served every year by the staff of *All Things Considered* and shared by everyone in the building who is working on that day. I come from a long line of groaning board Thanksgiving feasts, but the *ATC* dinner could match any one of them. It's not elegant — food arrives in plastic wrap and foil pans — but it's wonderful, and it's always huge.

The other theme you'll appreciate as you read (and I hope try) these recipes is that we are busy people. Like you, we don't have much time to prepare complicated dishes — almost everything in this book is easy and quick. Some of it, Bob Edward's Mint Julep recipe (p.76) for instance, is downright sudden. That's like a radio program as well. We try to pack as much news as we can into a few minutes, delivered just as fast and as fresh as we can manage. We offer this collection of recipes in the same spirit — with the addition of love, of course.

Linda Wertheimer, Senior National Correspondent

Contents

intros

Cajun Shrimp

Debbie Elliott, **Reporter**

This is a favorite appetizer and comes from my friend Susan. She served it one Christmas as the centerpiece of her table. She had taken one of those Styrofoam™ cones, covered it with pretty leaf lettuce, and then used toothpicks to stick the shrimp on it. It looked like a little decorated Christmas tree.

Boil water with lemon and cracked pepper, sea salt, cayenne pepper, mustard seeds, and bay leaf. Add shrimp. Cook 3 to 5 minutes. Drain and rinse. Peel and devein shrimp. (This is optional — I never devein!)

In large bowl, combine vegetable oil, olive oil, hot sauce, and spices. Beat with wire whisk. Pour over shrimp and toss. Cover and chill 4 to 8 hours. Drain and serve over leaf lettuce.

5 quarts water
1 large lemon, sliced
1 teaspoon each: cracked pepper, sea salt, cayenne pepper, and mustard seeds
1 bay leaf
5 pounds large shrimp
2 cups vegetable oil
1 tablespoon olive oil
1/2 cup hot sauce
2 tablespoons minced garlic
2 teaspoons salt
2 teaspoons seafood seasoning
1/4 cup chopped fresh basil
2 tablespoons chopped fresh oregano
2 tablespoons chopped fresh thyme
1/4 cup chopped fresh parsley
Leaf lettuce

Serves about 20

Ceviche de Almejas (Clam Ceviche)

Mandalit del Barco, **Reporter**

Dinners at my house have always been a Latin American feast, whipped up by Mom and Dad, Dolores and Renan del Barco. They're always in the kitchen together, dancing, laughing, and cooking with recipes handed down from Mom's Mexican-American relatives, and Dad's dishes from his native Peru. Once we immigrated to land-locked Kansas, they had to use canned baby clams instead of fresh fish to make ceviche. *¡Buen provecho!*

2 cups finely minced green onions
2 cans baby clams, drained
1 clove garlic, finely minced
Cilantro or parsley, minced
1 pinch oregano
Salt and pepper to taste
Juice from 3 limes
2 small chiles, finely chopped, optional

Serves 2

Mince the green onions and leave them soaking in cold, salted water while you prepare the other ingredients. Rinse and drain the onions and place them in a bowl. Add the remaining ingredients and mix well. Cover and place in refrigerator for at least 2 hours. Serve cold. Best with fresh salsa, boiled potatoes or potato chips, or *cancha* (roasted corn).

Chopped Eggplant

Lori Kaplan, **Research Manager**

This treasured and simple recipe was passed down through generations of Ukrainian relatives to my grandmother. She prepared it only for special Shabbos dinners. On one Friday night in 1969, this appetizer was the only food my mother ate. A few hours later, my brother Stephen was born. Unfortunately, my mother didn't think to share this story until after my two children were born — both three weeks past their due dates!

1 large eggplant
1 onion
Salt
Black pepper
Vegetable oil

Serves 3

Prick eggplant with a fork and bake in oven at 350 degrees for 1 hour. (Skin should be wrinkled.) Let it cool. After it cools, scrape out the inside and chop or mash with a fork. Throw away the skin.

Peel an onion and grate into chopped eggplant. Add some salt, a lot of black pepper, and some vegetable oil.

Cover with plastic wrap or aluminum foil and refrigerate. This can be served as an appetizer or can be spread on crackers or bread.

Cold Avocado Soup

Patt Morrison, **Commentator**

I was working in Mexico for a couple months on a project and it was difficult to find vegetarian dishes. Moreover, the weather was immensely warm. This was such a fresh, welcome change from hot and heavier starter foods. And hey, it's green, and the avocado is technically a fruit, so it's got to be good for you, right?

Slice the avocados and put them in a blender with two cups of the broth, lemon juice, salt, pepper, and a splash of hot sauce. Blend until it's smooth. (It looks like a facial masque, but resist the temptation!)

In a separate pan, over medium heat, combine butter and flour. Stir in the avocado mix, then add the remaining broth. Cook until it's smooth and thick. Add the sherry, the half and half, and onion and simmer for 20 minutes.

Season it to your liking, fussing with the right amounts of lemon juice, hot sauce, and the like. I like to make it the day before and refrigerate it overnight. When I serve it, I chill the bowls and garnish each serving with a bit of sour cream with a tortilla-chip "sail" stuck into it.

2 avocados, pitted
4 cups vegetable broth
Juice from half a lemon
1/2 teaspoon salt
1/4 teaspoon white pepper
4 tablespoons butter
2 tablespoons flour
1/2 cup sherry
2 cups half and half
1 tablespoon minced onion
Curry powder and/or hot sauce
Corn tortilla chips

Serves 4

Guacamole Soup with A Chipotle Dollop

Scott Simon, NPR News Host

Although I am widely advertised as having studied Mexican food at the feet of my esteemed friend, Rick Bayless (writer, chef, and expert on Mexican cuisine), this recipe is my own invention. It can be served hot or cold with just a minor adjustment for ingredients. I have served this soup to Rick, by the way. He seems to feel his future in Mexican food is still secure.

SOUP: Put avocado, garlic, salt, pepper, chopped onion, stock, and lemon juice into a blender. Blend on high until smooth and pale.

CHIPOTLE DOLLOP: Combine tomatoes, peppers, and pumpkin seeds or almonds in a small food processor (it will be tempting to use the blender again but the processor works best). Blend until the mixture is paste-like, with some coarse grain remaining. Put it into a bowl.

Ladle the soup into bowls. Using a small spoon, scoop the chipotle paste into a ball. Drop it — plop! — onto the pale green surface of the soup. Garnish with sprigs of cilantro. The dollop should melt as you stir, imparting a delightful spiciness. If you serve the soup hot, heat the pale green soup while adding a quarter cup of whole milk, or even cream. If you serve the soup cold, you could add a shot of tequila (in fact, you might do the same for the hot version), unless it's for a children's birthday party.

Soup

3 ripe avocados, pitted
2 cloves of garlic, smashed
Salt
Pepper
1 small onion, chopped
4 cups chicken or vegetable
    stock
Juice of 1 lemon

Chipotle Dollop

2 ripe plum tomatoes, chopped
2 chipotle chili peppers (canned
    is preferred – they're moist
    and plump)
1/4 cup pumpkin seeds or
    slivered almonds
Sprigs of cilantro

Serves 4

Horiatiki Salata

Maria Thomas, Vice President, NPR Online

When I was growing up, we had dinner at my Greek grandmother's house every Sunday. Dinner always started with meze, including a *horiatiki salata*. A *horiatiki salata*, the real Greek salad, is named for *Horiatiki* [of the village] + *salata* [salad]. It contains no lettuce, is heavy on the oregano, and is best eaten with French bread. Cut the bread into small pieces and let them sink to the bottom of the bowl where they absorb succulent juices and olive oil. Makes for beautiful skin and passionate dancers.

3 medium tomatoes
1 cucumber
1/2 medium onion
1 green bell pepper
1/2 pound Kalamata olives
1/2 pound Greek feta cheese
2 tablespoons virgin Greek
  olive oil
1/4 teaspoon white vinegar
1 tablespoon dried oregano
1 teaspoon dried mint
French bread

Serves 4

Cut tomatoes into 8 to 12 sections each. Peel cucumber (European/English style preferred) and slice into 1/4-inch thick slices. Peel and slice onion into 1/8-inch thick slices, cut each slice in half, and separate the onion layers. Peel and core pepper. Remove seeds and cut into 1/4-inch strips. Rinse olives to remove brine. Cut feta into 1/2-inch wide cubes and place in separate bowl. Mix all ingredients (except cheese) in a large salad bowl. Add feta last to avoid crumbling.

Mix in olive oil, vinegar, oregano, and mint in equal amounts, mixing in between (otherwise the spices cluster up). Chill for 1 hour. Serve chilled with fresh bread.

Hummus

Joanne Garlow, **Programmer, NPR Online**

When my husband and I lived in Istanbul we ate a lot of hummus. This very non-traditional recipe is adapted from Gabe Mirkin, and it has the advantage of being low in fat and high in garlic. It is a big hit at parties, because there is no guilt at all in this dip. Serve with pita bread and/or vegetables. This can be made in advance and refrigerated for up to a couple weeks.

Throw everything except the tomatoes in a food processor. You can add more garlic if you prefer — I think you really can't add too much garlic. Add about half of the tomatoes and blend until smooth. If it is too thick, add a little more tomato until you are happy with the consistency. Taste and adjust the proportions accordingly.

1 16-ounce can chickpeas
1/4 cup fresh-squeezed lemon juice
4 to 6 cloves garlic, minced
1/4 cup fresh parsley, leaves only
1 tablespoon cumin
1/4 to 1/2 teaspoon cayenne pepper
1 teaspoon paprika
Salt and pepper to taste
1 8-ounce can of tomatoes, crushed or whole

Serves 3 to 4

Lucia's Cornbread

Kevin Kling, **Commentator**

Lucia is a friend of mine, and she has a restaurant here in Minneapolis called Lucia's. She uses ingredients from the area and makes Midwest cooking seem downright epicurean. This is from her cookbook called *Savoring the Seasons of the Northern Heartland* by Beth Dooley and Lucia Watson. It's cornbread like you know it's supposed to taste. It's simple (important for me) and delicious. I guarantee it.

1 cup cornmeal
1 cup all-purpose flour
1/2 cup sugar
1 tablespoon baking powder
1/4 teaspoon salt
1 cup buttermilk
1 large egg
1/3 cup butter, melted

Makes 12 muffins or 12 pieces of cornbread

Preheat oven to 375 degrees. Sift the dry ingredients into a medium-sized bowl. Add the remaining ingredients and stir with a wooden spoon until the dry ingredients are just moistened. Do not overmix.

Spoon batter into muffin tins that have been lightly greased or filled with paper liners (or into a greased pan or cast iron skillet).

Bake for 15 to 20 minutes or until the centers of the muffins feel firm to the touch and a toothpick inserted in the center comes up clean. Cool 5 minutes before turning from the muffin tin, and serve warm.

Mexican Corn Salad

Gay Williams, **Budget Manager, Programming**

Whenever I ask my friends what to bring for a gathering, they frequently say, "something spicy and crunchy." My family and I were going to a friend's Fourth of July cookout and I didn't want to bring the same pasta salad. I thumbed through the many cookbooks I've collected over the years and found this recipe. Of course, I added a few more vegetables, herbs and spices to make it festive, cool, spicy, and crunchy — the culinary characteristics my friends love.

Put all the ingredients in a bowl, add olive oil and toss. Add salt and pepper to taste. Chill for 1 hour. Serve with tortilla chips and sour cream.

4 cups corn, fresh or canned, drained
1 can black beans, drained
1 cup chopped tomatoes
1 cup cilantro, chopped
1 cup green pepper, chopped
1 cup red pepper, chopped
1/2 cup red onion, chopped
1/2 cup green onion, chopped
4 tablespoons olive oil
Salt and pepper to taste

Serves 8 to 10

Party Pinwheels

Barbara Sopato, **E-Commerce Manager, NPR Online**

I thought if I ever had the opportunity to submit a recipe into a cookbook, it would most definitely be my recipe for deviled eggs. I believe deviled eggs are one of the most underrated American staple party foods, and I religiously serve them at every party I host.

    This is my second favorite appetizer. The great thing about these pinwheels is that they not only look cool, they can be prepared ahead of time and the recipe is easy to personalize, depending on your taste. These are always the first hors d'oeuvre to go — unless, of course, you're serving deviled eggs!

1 8-ounce package cream cheese, softened
1 cup sour cream
1 cup shredded Monterey Jack cheese
1/4 cup minced onion
1/2 teaspoon seasoned salt
1/4 teaspoon garlic powder
2 15-ounce cans black beans, drained
5 10-inch flour tortillas
Salsa, guacamole, or diced tomatoes for garnish

Serves 10 to 12

Combine cream cheese and sour cream; mix well. Stir in Monterey Jack cheese, onion, salt, and garlic powder. Chill 2 hours.

Purée beans in food processor or blender. Spread each tortilla with a thin layer of beans. Spread cream cheese mixture over beans, but not completely to the edge of the tortilla (the filling will ooze forward as you roll up the tortilla up).

Roll tortilla up tightly. Wrap in plastic wrap; chill for at least 2 hours (preferably overnight). Remove plastic and cut into 3/4-inch slices. Serve, pinwheel side up, with a dollop of salsa, guacamole or diced tomatoes.

Quick Onion Soup

Daniel Pinkwater, **Commentator**

This is suitable for an intimate lunch, or if your employer, clergyman, or U.S. senator should drop by. It's a masterpiece and it never fails. You can put on that Offenbach CD and listen while you slurp. I described this favorite recipe to my French relations when I visited Paris. They expressed amazement.

Heat the soup in a saucepan until it is hot, if that's how you like it. At the same time toast a slice of whole wheat bread in the toaster (or more if you're serving others). Here's the elegant touch: When the toast is done, cut it into bite-size squares.

Serve soup in a bowl or large cup and dump in the squares of toast (or croutons, for the effete).

Sprinkle with grated cheese.

Canned onion soup (as many as you need for the number of guests)
Sliced whole wheat bread
Grated cheese (Parmesan, Romano, your choice)

About 1 cup per person

Rhoda's Spinach Balls

Margaret Low Smith, **Vice President, Programming**

My mother, Natalie, had strong opinions about almost everything —
including food. When I was 6, I remember her coming home from
a party. I was already in bed and she came in to kiss me goodnight.
"How was the party?" I asked. "Lovely," she said, "but there wasn't
enough food. You should ALWAYS have too much food."

My mother was a wonderful cook and hostess. Her food was abundant, delicious, and elegant. For her baby sister, Rhoda, measuring up
in the kitchen was a deeply held aspiration. Rhoda was in her 30s the
first time she got the nerve to fix my mom dinner. She was anxious
and fretful — determined to win her big sister's approval. The food was
a hit and mom welcomed Rhoda into an exclusive club of people she
considered "fine" cooks.

Rhoda is in her 70s now and is a master in the kitchen. Her
spinach balls are one of my favorites. Mom adored them, too, and
insisted that Rhoda serve them on every possible occasion. For me they
are a testament to sisterly love and a shared passion for food and family.

2 10-ounce boxes chopped
    frozen spinach
4 eggs, beaten
1 large onion, finely chopped
3/4 cup melted butter
1/2 teaspoon garlic salt
3 or 4 teaspoons dried thyme
1/2 cup grated Parmesan
2 cups herb-flavor dry
    stuffing mix

Serves 4 to 6

Preheat oven to 350 degrees. Cook chopped spinach and squeeze dry. Mix
spinach, eggs, onion, and butter. Add garlic salt, thyme, grated Parmesan,
and stuffing mix. Mix well. Refrigerate at least 1 hour or overnight. Make
small balls on a cookie sheet and bake for 15 minutes.

Spinach Tourta

Kee Malesky, **Reference Librarian**

In the early 1900s, my great-grandfather, Luigi Gardella and his wife, Rosa, left the village of Neirone in the hills above Genoa, Italy, and came to New York. My great-grandmother, whom we always called "Nonna," brought along many recipes, including this one. My aunt Millie told me that *tourta* was the Genoese-dialect word for "toss." They call it that because you really have to mix and mix to get the ingredients properly combined.

2 cups rice
4 cups water
1 tablespoon butter
1/4 cup olive oil
1 8-ounce package cream cheese, softened
5 eggs
2 10-ounce packages frozen chopped spinach
1-1/2 cups Parmesan cheese

Serves 6 to 8

Preheat oven to 350 degrees. Cook rice in salted water. Thaw spinach and squeeze out the water. When rice is done, add butter and oil. When it cools slightly, add cream cheese. Let it cool more, and then add eggs (save a bit to brush on top), spinach, and Parmesan. Mix really well — mix until your arm hurts.

Spread in 9 x 13-inch roasting pan that has been oiled and sprinkled with breadcrumbs on all sides. Bake for 45 minutes or until the top is lightly browned. Cool and cut into squares.

To make a smaller *tourta*, halve the ingredients and bake in an 8-inch square pan. Serve warm or at room temperature. It reheats very well in the microwave.

Succulent Shrimp

John Ydstie, **Correspondent/Host**

Truth be told, this is my mother-in-law Ida's succulent shrimp, but it's so easy and tasty even I've made it with great success. If you must peel your shrimp before eating, don't forget to suck the spices off the shell first. I often eat the shrimp whole — peels, tails, and all. Yum-yum. But don't forget to floss. And remember: these are just guidelines. Stick with the amount of salt and chili powder, oil, and garlic that suits your taste buds.

Heat a big frying pan or wok over high heat. Add a tablespoon of oil and toss in 5 or 6 thin slices of garlic. Stir briefly until the garlic starts to turn golden (it will cook quickly). When the garlic is golden, add the salt and chili powder and mix with the garlic.

Add the shrimp and stir-fry until they begin to curl and turn bright orange. Don't cook too long. As you're cooking batches of shrimp, add oil, salt, and chili powder as necessary. Don't overdo the oil. Remove cooked shrimp to a separate platter.

Sprinkle the chopped cilantro over the shrimp, squeeze juice from a couple of the lime quarters and arrange the remaining limes on the platter for individual use or garnish.

Oil (It's best to use peanut oil because it can withstand high temperatures, but sometimes I use olive oil for the taste.)
6 to 8 cloves garlic, sliced
1/4 teaspoon salt (or to taste)
1/8 teaspoon chili powder
1 to 1-1/2 pounds medium to large uncooked shrimp, in the shell
1 to 2 bunches of coarsely chopped cilantro, stems removed
2 limes, quartered

Serves 6 to 8

Taleggio-stuffed Mushrooms

Scott M. Davis, **Manager, Corporate Sponsorship**

This is a recipe with special memories for me. I learned it 7 years ago so that I could cook for a woman I was falling for (I wanted to do something impressive). I think it worked — we've been married for nearly 3 years, and she requests this dish on a regular basis.

Preheat oven to 425 degrees. Wash and drain mushrooms. Remove stems and set caps aside. Chop enough of the stems to make 2 cups. In a medium saucepan cook chopped stems, onion, peppers, garlic, and oregano or basil in butter for 4 to 5 minutes, or until tender, stirring often. Remove from heat. Stir in the cheese and breadcrumbs.

Spoon about 1 tablespoon of the crumb mixture into each mushroom cap, pressing lightly. Arrange mushrooms in a 15 x 10 x 1-inch baking pan. Bake, uncovered, for 8 to 10 minutes or until mushrooms are heated through. Serve warm.

24 large fresh mushrooms, about 2 inches in diameter
1/4 cup finely chopped onion
2 tablespoons chopped green or sweet red pepper (combining both works, too)
1 clove garlic, minced
1/2 teaspoon dried oregano or basil, crushed
2 tablespoons butter
3/4 cup thinly sliced taleggio (you can substitute shredded provolone or fontina if you'd like)
1/4 cup dry Italian breadcrumbs

Serves 6

Ultimate Schorr Latke Synthesis

Daniel Schorr, **Senior News Analyst**

Potato pancakes, called *latkes*, are traditionally served during Hanukkah celebrations. I chose this recipe because it's something that unites my family. Every year at Hanukkah my kids ask, "Where are the *latkes*?" So, it's not only a delicious food, but part of a family tradition (with contributions from three generations of Schorrs: Tillie, Lisbeth B., Jonathan, and Lisa).

Grate the potatoes and onions together in food processor (do this in batches if necessary). Combine the potato and onion mixture in a bowl with the eggs, matzoh meal, salt, and baking powder. Mix all ingredients together well. When the ingredients are blended, put the mixture into a sieve to drain the moisture.

While this is draining, heat 1/4-inch of oil in a large frying pan. When the oil is very hot (test by splashing a drop of water into the pan; if it sizzles, it's hot enough), put large spoonfuls of the mixture into the hot oil, far enough apart so they don't touch. When one side is brown, turn pancakes over to brown the other side. Remove when browned on both sides and drain on paper towels.

If you're making large batches, they'll reheat best if you fry them again briefly in hot oil.

The custom is to serve *latkes* with sour cream and applesauce.

5 pounds potatoes
   (about 6 cups)
4 small or 3 large onions
   (about 1-1/2 cups chopped)
6 eggs
6 tablespoons matzoh meal
1 tablespoon salt
1-1/2 teaspoons baking powder
Cooking oil (your choice)
Sour cream
Applesauce

Serves 6

Yellow Squash Crisps

Roy Blount, Jr., **Panelist**, *Wait Wait ... Don't Tell Me!*

We didn't call these "crisps" when my mother made them when I was growing up. We called them "fried squash." But "crisps" has a nice cookbook-y ring to it, doesn't it? And they are crispy. But not just crispy — they're much finer as to texture and taste. I'd like to have some right now.

3 or 4 small-to-medium
yellow squash
Cooking oil (your choice)
1 cup cornmeal
Pinch of salt

Serves 4 to 6

Wash and cut the squash into thin round slices and set aside on a paper towel to "sweat." Heat 1/4-inch of oil in a heavy, seasoned-over-the-years cast iron skillet. While your oil is heating, put the cornmeal and a smidgen of salt (adjust to taste) into a paper bag and shake it to mix. Put the squash slices into the paper bag and shake to coat them.

Flick a little cornmeal into the oil to see if it's hot. If it sizzles fairly fiercely as if resenting the intrusion, start removing the cornmeal-coated slices of squash (they'll be mostly covered with the meal but not thickly) from the bag. Place one by one, side by side into the oil. As they brown, remove from heat and drain on a paper towel. Add more oil as needed (the oil doesn't have to be constant depth or temperature, as long as it's sizzling and lubricating).

Use elbows to keep anyone else in the kitchen from eating more than 5 percent of the finished crisps — and they'll try.

Main Features

Main Features

Avenue A Chicken

Vertamae Grosvener, **Correspondent**

I started making this chicken dish when I lived on Avenue A in New York. It quickly became a family favorite. It tastes best made the day before. Whenever my daughter Kali gets nostalgic for New York, she comes over and begs me to make this dish. Serve this over rice and with a green salad. It's wonderful.

In a large skillet over medium heat, melt the butter with the olive oil. Add the chicken and brown on both sides. Transfer the chicken to a plate.

Add the onion, bell pepper, celery, and garlic to the pan and sauté for 3 or 4 minutes. Stir in the olives, pimentos, tomatoes, and paprika. Return the chicken to the pan and season with salt and pepper.

Cover, reduce heat to low, and cook until the chicken is tender, about 35 to 40 minutes, turning the chicken once or twice.

1 tablespoon unsalted butter
1 tablespoon olive oil
1 chicken, cut into serving pieces
1 large onion, chopped
1/2 green or red bell pepper, seeded and chopped
1 stalk celery, chopped
2 to 3 cloves garlic, minced
1/4 cup pimento-stuffed green olives, sliced
1 small jar chopped pimentos
1 14-ounce can chopped tomatoes with juice
1/2 teaspoon paprika
Salt and freshly ground pepper to taste

Serves 4

Baccala Mantecato (Creamed Codfish)

Sylvia Poggioli, **Correspondent**

When many people think of Italian food, they think of pasta. Italian cuisine is one of the most varied in the world and I'd like to share with you the recipe of one less well-known specialty. It is just one of many Venetian ways of serving cod, a fish closely intertwined with the history of both Europe and New England. My mother was Venetian, and I was born and grew up in New England, so I am closely tied to this dish. This dish can be served as an appetizer or as a main course.

2 pounds salt cod
1 clove garlic
1-1/2 cups extra virgin olive oil
1 cup milk

Serves 4

Soak salt cod in water for 24 hours, changing the water often. Rinse in cold water; remove skin. Steam cod for 30 minutes to 1 hour. Remove fish from the heat and cool. Flake fish when cool. Remove bones and sinews. Place in food processor with the garlic clove and blend. With machine running, slowly add olive oil and milk; process until smooth.

Serve *baccala mantecato* hot or at room temperature with polenta. For centuries, polenta — the staff of life in the Veneto region and much of Northern Italy — was cooked through a laborious process in an unlined copper pot hanging from a hook in the center of a large fireplace, large enough to accommodate family members sitting on benches. Today there is a much less picturesque but much easier way to make polenta: Use instant polenta, which you can find in stores that sell Italian specialties.

Barbecue Meatloaf

Jack Speer, **Correspondent**

This recipe — thanks, Mom! — originated in Titusville, Pa., birthplace of the oil industry in Pennsylvania. Our family spent three years in Titusville in the late 1960s.

Preheat oven to 350 degrees. Mix together beef, bread crumbs, onion, beaten egg, salt, and half of 1 can of tomato sauce. Form into a loaf and put in shallow pan. Combine the rest of the tomato sauce, water, vinegar, brown sugar, prepared mustard, and Worcestershire sauce. Pour over loaf. Bake for 75 minutes, basting occasionally.

1-1/2 pounds ground beef
1 cup bread crumbs
1 onion, finely chopped
1 egg
1-1/2 teaspoons salt
2 8-ounce cans tomato sauce
1/2 cup water
3 tablespoons vinegar
3 tablespoons brown sugar
2 tablespoons prepared mustard
2 teaspoons Worcestershire
    sauce

Serves 4 to 6

Beef Stew

Nora Raum, **Newscaster**

We don't eat much red meat in our house, but I make an exception every St. Patrick's Day with a nod to my late mother, the former Clare Ann McNichols. I've adapted her version of beef stew — over the years, for example, I've added beer, which provides a rich, dark broth.

Dredge beef in flour, salt, and pepper while heating a large pot with a little oil in the bottom. Brown floured beef and add onion. Cook until onion is softened. Open the bottle of beer, drink one good slug, and then pour the rest into the pot. Simmer for approximately 15 minutes. Add potatoes and carrots, cover with beef broth, add salt and pepper, and simmer 1 hour or more until beef is tender.

2 pounds beef, cubed
1/2 cup flour (or more if necessary)
2 to 3 tablespoons vegetable or olive oil
1 large onion, diced
1 bottle cold, dark beer
4 large potatoes, cubed
3 carrots, diced
3 14-ounce cans beef broth
Salt and pepper

Serves 4 to 6

Calamari Pronto

Joanne Silberner, **Correspondent**

I learned to cook squid one summer in college. I worked at the Marine Biological Laboratory in Woods Hole, Mass., where I was trying to isolate yolk proteins from sea worms. One of my lab mates was so sick of pulling the nerves out of squid all day, she gave me all her nicely cleaned carcasses. The best thing about this dish is that if you have all the ingredients (or reasonable facsimiles) you can sit down and eat about 10 minutes after you walk in the door. Eat, enjoy, and be glad you don't have to use sea worms.

Put calamari in boiling water for a couple of minutes, then drain. Heat olive oil in a pan. Add garlic and sauté until golden. Lightly toast the pine nuts and add them to the oil, along with the pickled lemon. Add the drained calamari rings and salt or soy sauce. Cook a minute, stirring occasionally. Pour hot mixture over arugula or baby spinach; the greens will wilt beautifully. This recipe will tolerate a lot of creativity — try it with pepper flakes, or scallops.

8 ounces frozen calamari (squid) rings
2 to 3 tablespoons olive oil
4 cloves garlic, crushed and diced
1/4 cup pine nuts (pignoli)
1/2 large pickled lemon, or a whole small one, chopped into short thin slivers
1/2 teaspoon salt or soy sauce to taste
4 cups arugula or baby spinach

Serves 2

Corley Slam

Cheryl Corley, **Reporter**

This meal began on an evening when I came home starving. "What to eat?" There was nothing much left in the fridge, the cupboards looked lonely, grocery day was near. Thus began the Corley Slam, a quick rendition of "Let's cook whatever is in the house." Throw it over rice or eat it as is. People who swear they don't like vegetables always eat this and ask for more — plus you can name it after yourself — after all, you're the one doing the slammin'.

Onions
Green peppers
Mushrooms
Tomatoes
Leftover chicken or ham
Canned or frozen vegetables
Olive oil
Seasonings

Approximately 3/4 cup per person, when served over rice

Slice and sauté the onions, green peppers, mushrooms, and tomatoes. Slice the chicken or ham. Defrost your veggies in the microwave or open the can and drain the liquid.

Slam it all in the pan and stir fry. Add whatever seasonings you like, but my staples are onion powder, garlic powder, pepper, and seasoning salt.

Davar's Persian Kotlets

Davar Ardalan, **Producer**

One of my favorite pastimes with my daughter Samira is to make *kotlets* **(burgers). It's almost as fun as shopping and has none of that pesky buyer's remorse. These are fun and versatile because they can be an actual meal if you make a side dish of rice, or you can take them on picnics and eat them cold with** *lavash* **bread and pickles.**

My grandmother, who has always been a fabulous cook, judged us by our ability to make a good kotlet and I have her seal of approval on these. You can also double the recipe, make two dozen at a time, and freeze them (wrap each *kotlet* **in wax paper) to cook at your leisure. They are simply divine!**

1 pound ground beef
1 medium onion, minced
2 cloves of garlic, minced
3 medium potatoes, boiled, peeled, and mashed
1 egg
Dash turmeric
Dash cinnamon
Dash lemon pepper
Dash salt
1-1/2 cups breadcrumbs

Makes 10 to 12 *kotlets*

Preheat oven to 375 degrees. Combine ground beef with onion, garlic, potatoes, egg, and spices. Form into oval patties and pat them in breadcrumbs on both sides.

Spray a cookie sheet with oil and place the patties on the sheet. Cook in oven for 20 minutes, turn them over and cook for another 15 or until crisp on both sides. These taste wonderful served with cucumber and tomato salad.

End of Moose Season Beans

Corey Flintoff, **Newscaster**

This refers not to the end of moose-hunting season but to the end of moose-eating season. It's for that time when you've dug down to the bottom of the freezer and there's not one odd-shaped, badly labeled package of moose meat left. Or, it's for when there are still way too many of those packages, and you just can't face another moose burger, moose kebab, moose hash, or moose vindaloo. This dish is the handiwork of my wife, Diana Derby.

Rinse beans well and soak overnight (check for rocks). Drain and rinse again. Put beans in a big pot with enough water to cover, about 1 to 2 inches. Bring to a boil and lower heat to simmer with lid askew for 3 to 4 hours. Check and add water as needed until beans are soft.

Sauté diced vegetables and garlic in olive oil. Add vegetables, crushed tomatoes, and tomato paste to cooked beans, simmer another hour. Chop spinach very fine, so it's almost like an herb, and add to beans. Crumble soy meat directly into beans (it's already cooked).

Add hot sauce, tequila, salt, and pepper to taste.

1 16-ounce bag beans, either black or small red beans
2 to 3 tablespoons olive oil
1 each medium-sized onion, red pepper, yellow pepper, carrot
2 teaspoons minced garlic
1 28-ounce can crushed tomatoes
1 small can tomato paste
1 cup chopped frozen or 2 cups fresh spinach
1 12-ounce package veggie ground round-style soy meat (Mexican Seasoned)
2 tablespoons Louisiana-style hot sauce
2 tablespoons tequila (you decide about the worm)
Salt and pepper to taste

Serves 6 to 8

Finnan Haddie Delmonico

Richard Knox, **Correspondent**

Finnan haddie is a Scottish dish. "Finnan" originally referred to haddock from the Scottish fishing port of Findon. My history with this dish begins in a suite at the Boston Ritz-Carlton where my wife, Jean, and I celebrated our honeymoon. I've tried other versions, but the following, slightly modified from a Craig Claiborne recipe in the 1961 *New York Times Cookbook,* is the best. This is not a difficult dish, unless your mashed potatoes are too stiff or too runny.

Preheat oven to 400 degrees. Make mashed potatoes and set aside. Place the fish in a shallow pan, cover with water and simmer for 15 minutes. Drain and cool the fish. Flake fish into large pieces, removing bones and skin. Melt butter and add flour and whisk until blended. Bring the milk to a boil and add, all at once, to the butter-flour mixture, stirring vigorously with the whisk until the roux is thickened and smooth. Season with salt and pepper.

Add the fish and eggs to the roux and mix carefully to avoid mashing the fish. Pour the mixture into a casserole. Put mashed potatoes into a pastry tube with a large fluted tip and pipe rosettes on top of the fish mixture. This is tedious, but it makes for a classy presentation. Sprinkle with grated cheese and bake until the top is golden brown. The dish can hold in the refrigerator, uncooked, overnight. Bake just before serving.

2 cups mashed potatoes (not too stiff, but not runny)
1-1/2 pounds of finnan haddie (smoked haddock)
1-1/4 cup butter
3 tablespoons flour
2 cups whole milk
Salt and freshly ground black pepper
4 hard-boiled eggs, quartered
Grated Parmesan cheese

Serves 4 to 6

Fish & Pineapple Soup

Jackie Northam, **Reporter**

I lived overseas for a number of years, at one point in Cambodia. The BBC correspondent and I shared a beautiful French Colonial house near the Royal Palace. As part of the rental contract we agreed to hire several of the owners' friends. We ended up with a cleaner who couldn't clean, a cook who couldn't cook, and a guard who, on two occasions, watched helplessly as thieves stole vehicles parked in our driveway. Never mind. We sent our cook, Pinny, for cooking lessons and she learned two dishes. This is one of them.

Heat the oil in a large pot. Sauté garlic, lemongrass, chili, and onion. Stir in tomatoes. Cook for a couple of minutes. Add water, fish stock, fish sauce, tamarind paste, sugar, pineapple, and lime juice. Cook for 10 minutes. Add fish and cook for another 10 minutes or until fish is tender. Transfer to soup bowls and garnish with basil.

1 tablespoon vegetable oil
2 cloves garlic, minced
1 stalk lemongrass, minced
2 to 3 small red chilies
2 small onions, chopped
4 medium tomatoes, seeded and chopped
3 cups water
2 cups fish stock
2 tablespoons fish sauce
1 tablespoon tamarind paste
1 to 2 teaspoons sugar
1 cup pineapple, chopped
2 tablespoons lime juice
1 pound firm white fish, cut into bite-size pieces
1/2 cup fresh basil leaves, chopped

Serves 6

Girl From Ipanema Mussels

Alphonse Vinh, **Reference Librarian**

I've named this recipe after one of my favorite Bossa Nova songs. One of my cousins, Marie-Christine, lives with her husband and children in the northern French city of Lille. Each fall, the city organizes a weekend *braderie,* a street fair in the old town. The festival also celebrates *moules frites,* which some say is the national dish of Belgium and the municipal favorite of Lille — steamed mussels with french fries. Here's my version, which I always make at Christmas.

Heat the oil on high in a *cazuela* or large stockpot. Add garlic and sauté until golden. Add the wine, bay leaf, lemon juice, pepper, and sea salt. Simmer, covered, for 5 minutes.

Add the mussels to the sauce, cover, and cook until the mussels open up. Sprinkle with the cilantro, briskly shake the pot, and gently simmer the mussels for just a short time.

Serve with slices of toasted country bread.

4 pounds live mussels
2 tablespoons extra-virgin olive oil
2 cloves garlic, finely minced
2 cups dry white wine
1 bay leaf
2 tablespoons fresh lemon juice
Freshly ground pepper
Sea salt
1 tablespoon minced cilantro
Sliced baguette or country bread

Serves 6 to 8

Green Bean Burritos

Emily Harris, **Reporter**

This came about because I was usually starving by the time I got home when I lived in Washington, D.C. In Berlin now, I live at the office. I love to eat food wrapped up in bread and I never get enough green vegetables. Spearing green beans one by one with a fork is a lot less appetizing to me than munching them in a sandwich!

One night my charming husband asked me what I would like for dinner and I said "green bean burritos" and described exactly what I wanted. He kindly obliged and I now consider it one of his specialties. I've only cooked it once myself — though I usually clean the beans and I am supposed to wash the dishes.

Fresh green beans (how many depends on how hungry you are)
1 tablespoon olive oil
1 medium onion, chopped
Garlic, chopped or minced
1 or 2 red peppers, diced
10-inch tortillas
Thai hot sauce, optional

Wash green beans and break or cut off the stems. Heat oil in a pan and add onion and garlic. Sauté until golden. Add the green beans and cook until they start to turn brighter green (don't cook the beans too much — the key is that they are still a little crunchy). Add the red pepper and cook until softened. Roll it up in a tortilla and eat.

Heartbreak Pizza

Brenda Wilson, **Correspondent/Editor**

This is the thing to make when your heart has been broken and you're thousands of miles from home. This remedy was prepared for me by good friends Ryan Seddon and Hugh Cross, the son and nephew of friends for whom I was house-sitting in Johannesburg. This should not be eaten alone. It requires the hand-holding of two to three friends who are still young enough to be mystified why the loss of three minutes in a story could occasion such heartbreak. The first ingredient is a bottle of Irish whiskey — it stops the sobbing almost immediately.

Preheat oven to 350 degrees. To get the demons out, fiercely chop tomatoes, onion, garlic, green pepper, and parsley. In a saucepan, heat olive oil. Add 2/3 of the onion and garlic. Sauté until golden. Mix in 2/3 of the tomatoes. Add the tomato paste, thyme, and oregano. Stir and simmer.

Cover the pizza dough with the cooked sauce, and the remaining 1/3 uncooked ingredients, cheese, and whatever else is in your refrigerator. In my case it was provolone, chicken morsels, pineapple, chutney, sprinkling of garlic, cayenne, and green peppers. Bake until cheese starts to bubble, 15 to 20 minutes.

Dance.

1 prepared pizza dough
2 tablespoons olive oil
5 tomatoes
1 medium onion
2 or 3 cloves of garlic
1 green pepper
1 bunch parsley
2 tablespoons tomato paste
2 teaspoons each thyme and oregano
Mozzarella or Provolone cheese

Serves 4 to 6

Homemade Pizza Crust

Patricia Neighmond, **Correspondent**

About two years ago, our neighbors invited us to dinner for "home-made" pizza. I was skeptical. Although I have fond memories of thick-crusted, cheese-drenched Chicago-style pizza, I have been trying to remain "California-lite" in recent years. So, I was pleasantly surprised when presented with an extremely thin-crusted (which must mean fewer calories) pizza that can be decorated with luscious lower-fat items such as goat cheese, sun-dried tomatoes, Kalamata olives, etc.

1 teaspoon active dry yeast
1/2 cup lukewarm water or milk
1/4 teaspoon salt
1 teaspoon olive oil
1-1/4 cups flour

Enough for an 8- to 10-inch
pizza

Sprinkle the yeast into the water or milk. Let stand 5 minutes. Add salt, oil, and half the flour and beat for 2 minutes with a wooden spoon. Add remaining flour, stirring, and then kneading, as you go. The dough will be soft. Turn out and knead on a floured board for 5 minutes. Oil the bowl, put the dough back in, and let rise for 1 hour.

The dough is now ready to use. If you want to store it for a few days, divide it in half, put it in a plastic container with a lid and refrigerate or freeze. Thaw thoroughly before using.

TOPPINGS: One of our favorites is portobello mushroom and Parmigiano-Reggiano cheese: Cover pizza with shredded cheese. Add sliced mushrooms, sliced leeks, sliced garlic. Top with shredded fresh thyme. Bake at 500 degrees for 10 to 15 minutes, or until edges are brown and crispy. Remove from oven and sprinkle with white truffle oil.

Ia's Delight

Lakshmi Singh, **Newscaster**

My great-aunt, Ia (pronounced EE-ah) was always the center of attention when it came to cooking in Ponce, Puerto Rico. People often visited her, knowing they'd get a great meal. Her kitchen was the gathering place, where the family managed to remain united, and new friends became part of our family. She recently passed away, but this dish is one very potent reminder of how precious she was to all of us — as a fabulous cook, a funny woman, and a great person.

Sauté all ingredients in part B for 10 minutes in a slightly heated pan. Allow to cool after 10 minutes.

In a bowl, put ingredients from part A — shrimp, scallops, crumbled bacon, cooked chicken breast cut in cubes, and sliced pieces of avocado. Add the mixture from part B and mix together well.

Add salt and pepper to taste.

Part A

1 pound shrimp, cooked, shelled, and deveined
1 pound cooked scallops
6 strips cooked bacon, crumbled
2 pieces boneless chicken breast, cooked
1 ripe avocado, peeled and sliced

Part B

1/2 cup olives, pitted
1/2 cup extra virgin olive oil
1/4 cup vinegar, apple or balsamic
1 onion, chopped
1 small can red pimentos
Salt and black pepper

Serves 4

Melanie's Chicken

Nina Totenberg, **Correspondent**

This was my mother's recipe and ever since has been known to all by her name.

Rub the chicken parts with garlic, then season with salt and pepper. Add soy sauce, slice of fresh ginger, and lemon juice. Make sure you have enough liquid to soak the chicken. Marinate overnight, flesh side down. Broil and serve with rice.

1 chicken, cut into parts
Garlic, minced
Salt and pepper
Soy sauce
Fresh ginger, sliced
Lemon juice

Serves 4

Nona's Pasta Fazul

Noah Adams, **Senior Correspondent**

This recipe comes from my wife, author and NPR producer Neenah Ellis: "Both my grandmothers were from islands off the coast of Croatia, a region known historically as Dalmatia. Culturally, it's more Italian than Slavic and as a result, many of their recipes are traditional Italian fare.

"My mother's mother, Giovanina Manghera (her father was born in Italy), came to Chicago around 1920. She had great flair, a wonderful sense of humor, and spoke fluent Italian and Croatian. I was her first granddaughter and namesake. I loved staying overnight with her and hearing her stories about the *stari kraj,* the old country, and sitting at her kitchen table. I can still see the cracked wooden spoon she would wave in the air as she urged me to 'Eat, eat!' (*Mangia, mangia!*) This is my favorite recipe of hers."

1 large onion
1 bunch celery
3 cloves garlic
Olive oil
1 large and 1 small can
    of tomato sauce
2 potatoes, diced
Pasta shells
1 15-ounce can kidney beans
Salt and pepper
Parmesan or Romano cheese,
    grated

Serves 4 to 6

Chop onion, celery, and garlic. Sauté in olive oil in a heavy pot. Add the tomato sauce. Add potatoes and 1/2 box of pasta shells. Cover all with hot water and boil on high until the pasta absorbs the water. Add kidney beans, salt, and pepper, and heat through. Serve with lots of grated Parmesan or Romano cheese.

Oven-fried Chicken

Adam Hochberg, **Correspondent**

When I graduated from college and went off to live on my own, my mother wrote out some of her old family recipes for me. She wrote them in longhand, including a generous amount of motherly advice tailored to somebody with little experience in the kitchen (i.e., "Some splattering may occur when liquid is added, so please lean away from skillet."). This was one of my favorite recipes as a child and even though it's a cholesterol buster, my wife and I still enjoy it today.

4 chicken breasts or one whole chicken, cut up
1 cup flour
1/2 teaspoon garlic powder
1 teaspoon seasoning salt
Vegetable oil or shortening

Serves 4

Combine flour, garlic powder, and seasoning salt in a large bowl or plastic bag. Coat the chicken in the mixture and let it sit on a plate in the refrigerator for a couple of hours.

Preheat oven to 425 degrees. In a baking pan with high sides, add about 1/4-inch of oil or shortening and heat in the oven. When the oil is hot, remove pan from oven and arrange floured chicken in a single layer, skin side down.

Bake uncovered 20 to 25 minutes or until it is golden brown. Turn over and bake another 20 minutes or until chicken is golden brown. Drain chicken on paper towels.

Pasta Diablo

John McChesney, **Correspondent**

I first learned the rudiments of this dish from Laurie Garrett, who used to report on science for NPR. The dish was a hit every time I made it and it's become part of my regular repertoire. I can't remember a single person who hasn't liked it — unless they were just being polite.

Some people shudder at the anchovies, but then are pleasantly surprised when they discover that the dish does not have a fishy flavor. Sometimes I overdo the red pepper and flame out some delicate palates.

Heat the oil over moderate heat and add the anchovies. With a little stirring they will dissolve into paste in the oil. Add the garlic and red pepper. Cook garlic until golden. Cook for a few minutes over low heat until the oil is fully flavored with the red pepper flakes.

Cook and drain pasta thoroughly. Place in a dish and top with the chopped basil or parsley (basil, by the way, gives it a more exciting flavor). Pour the sauce on top and toss relentlessly until everything is evenly distributed.

Do not use cheese on this recipe. It fights with the underlying anchovy base.

2 to 3 tablespoons olive oil
1 can anchovy filets
6 plump cloves garlic, crushed
   or minced
1 tablespoon red pepper flakes
   (or to taste)
1 box or less of #11
   pasta/spaghettini
1 bunch coarsely chopped basil
   or Italian parsley

Serves 4 to 6

Peanut Chicken Rolls

Liane Hansen, **NPR News Host**

When Neal Conan and I lived in London and our son was newborn, I needed to lose weight so I joined a weight loss group. This is an adaptation of one of its recipes. While the taste reminded me of home, peanut butter in England tastes different from its American cousin. In order to get American-style peanut butter, I shopped at Fortnum & Mason where it was in the "imported" ("expensive") section. So, what was a relatively cheap meal in the U.S. became a luxury dish in the U.K.

4 boneless chicken breasts, pounded flat
4 tablespoons peanut butter, creamy or crunchy, your choice
1 small sweet onion, chopped
1 or 2 teaspoons paprika
Butter

Serves 4

Preheat oven to 350 degrees. Mix together the peanut butter, onion, and some of the paprika. Put approximately 1 tablespoon of the mixture atop an uncooked chicken breast. Spread the mixture around a bit, then roll the breast up and secure with a toothpick. If you don't have toothpicks, just place the rolls seam-side down to bake.

Put the chicken rolls in a greased baking dish. Put 1 pat of butter on top of each breast and sprinkle with more paprika. Cover and bake for 20 to 30 minutes.

This tastes great with noodles or rice, and snap peas or green beans as side dishes.

Revisionist Salade Frisée aux Lardons

Daniel Zwerdling, **Correspondent**

My wife and I used to ask friends if they'd like to try this amazingly delicious and simple salad, inspired by one of my NPR reporting trips in France. Most would politely say, "No." Were they turned off by the fact that I would describe it as a "warm salad"? When I mentioned the lettuce would be draped with "runny poached eggs"? These days we serve it to our loved ones without asking. Sometimes it's a first course, but it's also satisfying as a light meal.

Chop the bacon in coarse chunks. Sauté in a heavy pan until it starts to brown. Turn off heat but keep bacon in the pan. Poach the eggs. When the eggs are almost done, pour the oil and vinegar into the still-hot pan with the bacon (if the pan has cooled, reheat for a moment). Swirl eggs around until they're hot but not smoking.

Quickly toss the lettuce with the vinaigrette and bacon (it should taste quite vinegary at this point) and salt and pepper. Divide among plates, then top each mound of salad with one or two hot poached eggs. Add a last grind of pepper for appearances' sake.

1 or 2 bunches arugula or escarole
4 eggs
1/2 pound low-fat bacon or fat-free turkey bacon
3 to 4 tablespoons red wine vinegar
1 or 2 tablespoons extra virgin olive oil
Salt and pepper to taste

Serves 4 to 6

Salmon Pasta Supreme

Tom Goldman, **Correspondent**

This recipe started in a book called *Dungeness Crabs and Blackberry Cobblers: The Northwest Heritage Cookbook* by Janie Hibler. We took a recipe she had for grilled sablefish with pasta, fresh basil, and red peppers and changed the sablefish to salmon. This is our reconstituted version.

Preheat oven to 375 degrees. Bake the salmon, skin side down, for about 20 minutes until the center is just opaque. Remove from oven and let sit to cool. Boil the pasta until it is firm but soft. Remove from heat and drain. Heat oil in a pan and sauté peppers and garlic until just softened and golden. Flake cooled salmon and toss with peppers, garlic, and basil and pasta. Mix in the olive paste and the avocado.

1 pound salmon filet
1 package penne pasta
4-1/2 tablespoons olive oil
2 garlic cloves, minced
1 cup chopped red pepper
1/2 heaping cup chopped fresh basil
3 heaping tablespoons olive paste
1 cup peeled and chopped avocado, optional

Serves 4 to 6

Salmon Steamed in Sake with Sake Butter

Fred Child, **Host**

I don't often go looking for things to do in the kitchen, but anything with the word "salmon" captures my attention. This turned out to be an amazingly quick and easy dish for a lazy guy like me. I adapted it from a recipe in *The New York Times*. As a bonus, it's stunningly delicious, full of bright summery flavor, and will fool your friends into thinking you are a great chef.

SALMON: Put water and sake into a pot (large enough to accomodate your vegetable steamer). Add lemongrass. Add a bit of shredded orange peel to the mix and stir for about a minute. Tear the rest of the orange peel into half a dozen pieces and toss into the sake and water mixture. Add ginger slices. Let simmer. Bring the mixture to a boil. Put vegetable steamer over pot, and lay the salmon on the steamer. Cover and steam for 3 to 4 minutes or longer for more well-done salmon.

SAKE BUTTER: Melt one tablespoon of butter in a saucepan with ginger and shallots under medium heat. When ginger and shallots are golden, add 1/2 cup sake and bring to a boil. Cook until mixture reduces to a few tablespoons. Add the butter chunks one by one and whisk until melted. Reduce heat to low. Stir in remaining one tablespoon of sake, lime juice and salt.

Serve salmon with sake butter spooned on top surrounded by lime wedges.

Steamed Salmon

2 pounds salmon filets, skinned and cut into four pieces
2 cups sake
2 cups water
1 stalk lemongrass, split lengthwise
1 orange peel
Fresh ginger, julienned into 12 thin slices
1 lime, cut into four wedges (for garnish)

Sake Butter

1 stick unsalted butter, chopped into about a dozen chunks (plus 1 tablespoon)
10 thin strips of fresh ginger
2 shallots, minced
1/2 cup sake, plus 1 tablespoon sake
2 teaspoons lime juice
Salt to taste

Serves 4

Seared Steak

Todd Holzman, **Senior Editor, NPR Online**

If I still ate red meat — or needed to feed someone who does — this is the foolproof recipe I would use to make an excellent steak without lighting a grill or dirtying a broiler pan. Turn on the range fan or open a kitchen window before you start.

1 tablespoon virgin olive oil
1 8-ounce N.Y. strip steak, 1/2 inch thick (per person)
10-inch iron skillet
White pepper

Serves 1

Heat the oil in the skillet — it must be an iron skillet. Allow the oil to become hot enough to sear the meat. Trim exterior fat from steak(s) and rub white pepper on both sides. When the pan is hot, carefully place the steak in the middle of the pan. Leave for 4 minutes without poking, prodding, or otherwise molesting the meat. The hot pan will seal in the juices of the meat.

After four minutes, carefully flip the steak and cook the other side for 4 minutes.

You now have a "medium" strip steak and possibly a modest amount of greasy smoke in your kitchen. Reduce the cooking time on each side by equal amounts if you like it more rare.

Shrimp & Feta Cheese

Steve Inskeep, **NPR News Host**

For years, my wife Carolee and I didn't have any money to speak of, so a lot of our meals came out of a box or a can. We ate lots of macaroni and cheese, or that Chinese food that comes in the two cans taped together. This was one of the first recipes Carolee cooked when we finally had enough money to buy fresh ingredients. It's a simple dish and not terribly expensive to make. It tasted good then, and it still tastes good now.

This dish cooks quickly so get everything prepared before you start.

Heat olive oil in an extra-large skillet over medium-high heat. Add tomatoes, pepper, and garlic. Sauté until the pepper is tender, about 3 to 5 minutes. Add shrimp and sauté until the shrimp is cooked through on both sides, about 3 to 5 minutes. Remove from heat.

Stir in oregano, hot pepper sauce to taste, and feta cheese. Transfer to plates.

2 or 3 tablespoons virgin olive oil

2 large tomatoes, pulp and seeds removed, chopped

1 bell pepper, seeds removed, chopped

1 tablespoon fresh garlic, chopped

2 pounds large shrimp, peeled and deveined

2 teaspoons dried oregano

Several dashes hot pepper sauce

1 generous cup crumbled feta cheese

Serves 4

Shrimp & Grits

Carl Kasell, **Newscaster**

I'm sorry to say that I have never cooked, do not cook now, and at my age, will probably never cook. I have had the fortune of having a mother who was a great Southern cook, a first wife who was a great Italian cook, and my second wife who is also a great cook. They have all had their own ways of putting together a delicious meal and I have learned to stay out of their way.

I am from the South (North Carolina), but I don't recall eating shrimp and grits until I ran across the dish at a restaurant in North Carolina a few years ago. There are many variations of this recipe, but this is the one we like.

Grits (not instant)
2 or 3 slices bacon
1 small onion, finely minced
1 pound shrimp, peeled and
    deveined
1 14-ounce can of crushed
    tomatoes
1/2 teaspoon hot pepper sauce

Serves 3 to 4

Prepare the grits according to the directions. True grits, prepared properly, take a long time to cook (try to avoid using instant grits). While grits are cooking, cut shrimp in half and set aside.

Cook bacon until it's crisp. Remove cooked bacon from the pan, drain most of the fat, add onions to the same pan and sauté until golden. When grits are nearly done, add halved shrimp, crumbled bacon and onions to the grits and stir. Finish cooking the grits.

When grits are done, add tomatoes and hot pepper sauce to taste. Mix well.

Sopa de Ajo (Garlic Soup)

David Welna, **Correspondent**

My wife Kathleen spent years living in Spain before relocating to Argentina, where we met. One of the reasons she enchanted me was her love for this wonderful comfort food meal-in-a-bowl she learned to make in Spain, where there are always plenty of day-old baguettes to slice up for the soup. This is very simple food, and it's hard to beat, if you love garlic.

Slice the loaf of bread into 3/4-inch rounds, then cut those rounds into quarters. Heat the olive oil over medium heat in a heavy pan large enough to hold all the ingredients. When the oil is warm, toss in the garlic and stir until it just begins to turn golden.

Toss in all the diced-up bread, and stir it around so it absorbs the olive oil. Continue until the garlic looks toasted, but not burnt. Add the chicken broth to the bread and garlic mixture. Lightly whip eggs in a bowl. Once the broth is simmering, add eggs and stir.

The soup is now done. Serve it in wide bowls, and have a pepper mill on hand for those who like a little more zing.

Half of a day-old (or older) baguette
8 cloves garlic, minced
1/3 cup extra virgin olive oil
4 cups chicken broth
2 eggs
Salt and ground black pepper to taste

Serves 4

Spaghetti alla Ombudsmani

Jeffrey Dvorkin, **Ombudsman**

My family and I used to rent summer houses in southern France and Italy when our son was quite young. We would buy fresh ingredients in the local market to make a fast supper on our balcony or the deck. After this dinner, we would go for a nice walk (*passegiatta*) and have a coffee and a cognac at the local cafe. A perfect summer meal in perfect surroundings.

In an oven heated to 200 degrees, place an empty serving dish containing 1 tablespoon of olive oil. Prepare the spaghetti in the usual way. Fry the onions until crisp in olive oil. Add the remaining ingredients and sauté for about 5 minutes or until the bacon is crispy.

Remove the serving dish from the oven. Drain the cooked spaghetti and pour into serving dish. Stir pasta around to coat in oil. Pile the cooked mixture on top and serve very hot with grated cheese.

1 pound whole wheat spaghetti (bigoli)
1/2 pound chopped onions
2 tablespoons olive oil
4 rashers/strips bacon cut into squares
1/4 pound chopped mushrooms (preferably morels, trompettes de la mort, or any other smoky-tasting kind)
2 cloves garlic, chopped
Handful of pitted Niçoise black olives
4 anchovy filets
Chopped parsley
Grated fresh Parmigiano-Reggiano cheese

Serves 4

Squid Pie

Ray Magliozzi, **Host**, *Car Talk*

This is an old Magliozzi family recipe, handed down from my grandmother to my mother to me. It always occupied a warm spot in our hearts — especially since it was the only one that wasn't responsible for killing off any family members.

In a large saucepan of boiling water, cook the squid for 5 minutes. Drain it and chop into small pieces. In a bowl combine the squid, olives, parsley, tomatoes, garlic, oil, crushed red pepper, and salt. Cover and marinate overnight in the fridge.

The next day, oil a 12-inch shallow baking dish. Set the oven at 400 degrees. Roll out half the dough and line the pan with it. Drain stuffing. This is important: Get rid of all the liquid or the bottom will get soggy. Put stuffing on the dough. Roll out the other piece of dough and cover the stuffing. Crimp the edges as you would a pie. Cut a few ventilation holes in the top so it doesn't explode. Rub some olive oil on your hands and pat the top.

Transfer the pie to the oven. It's done when the top and the bottom crusts are a golden brown, about 30 to 35 minutes (if it turns black, you blew it). Cool for 15 minutes before eating (if you can wait that long!).

Pizza dough (enough for two 12-inch pizzas)
2 pounds fresh squid, cleaned
3/4 cup black olives, chopped
3/4 cup Italian parsley, chopped
3 large fresh tomatoes, chopped
5 cloves garlic, chopped
1/4 cup olive oil
1/2 teaspoon crushed red pepper
1/2 teaspoon salt
Olive oil (for the top)

Serves 4

Swordfish Liasson

Mara Liasson, **Correspondent**

I think I saw this recipe in *The New York Times Magazine* years ago. I never actually clipped it, but I remembered the ingredients. I've been making it for years, and it's delicious. Here's a cooking tip: I use a grilling cage so that it's easier to flip the steaks over.

4 thick swordfish steaks
Dijon mustard, smooth
Soy sauce
Grated ginger, to taste

Mix mustard, soy sauce, and ginger and slather it all over the swordfish. Marinate for an hour. Grill the steaks about 10 minutes per side (the amount of time depends on your grill). Serve with grilled vegetables, salad, and rice.

Thai Chicken with Basil

Bob Mondello, **Correspondent**

When we go to Thai restaurants, I always order the spicy chicken with basil. When I saw a recipe for it in *The New York Times Magazine* one Sunday, I clipped it and dutifully assembled the ingredients. It called for fish sauce, which I'd never used before. It was awful and had a heavy fish flavor and odor. I substituted oyster sauce and have dined happily on this ever since.

Because it comes together quickly at the end, you'll want to get all the ingredients ready in advance (combine the oyster sauce, soy sauce, and sugar in a cup so you won't have to measure while stirring).

In a large frying pan, heat oil. Sauté garlic and peppers for about a minute over medium-high heat until the garlic starts to turn brown. Add chicken, stirring constantly until you see no more pink. Stir in oyster sauce, soy sauce, and sugar, and cook for about 1 minute, then taste (you may want to add a few drops more of oyster sauce). Add fresh basil leaves and remove from heat as soon as they start to wilt (about 30 seconds). Serve immediately over rice.

1 tablespoon olive oil
4 cloves crushed garlic
1 or 2 jalapeño peppers or
    1 teaspoon dried red
    pepper flakes
4 boneless chicken breast
    halves, sliced thinly
2 tablespoons oyster sauce
1 tablespoon soy sauce
1 teaspoon sugar
1 cup fresh basil leaves or
    1/4 cup dried basil flakes

Serves 4

Transylvanian Cabbage and Noodles

Andrei Codrescu, **Commentator**

As the marvelous smell of cabbage fills the house, bringing with it vivid memories of large immigrant families crowded in New York tenements, and the distant sound of wailing from the *shtetls* of Ukraine, read a preprandial I.B. Singer story.

Preheat oven to 350 degrees. Finely chop the head of cabbage and sauté in the butter with salt, pepper, and paprika. Boil until soft a package of flat egg noodles. Combine soft cabbages with limp noodles in a baking dish and bake together for 20 minutes. Serve with dollop of sour cream.

1 cabbage head
1 stick butter
Salt and pepper
5 tablespoons Hungarian
     paprika
1 package flat egg noodles
Sour cream

Serves 4

Welcome Home Salad

Alex Chadwick, **NPR News Host**

I made this salad for my wife, Carolyn Jenson, on the evening she returned from a very quick trip to Malaysia for a *Radio Expeditions*® story. She flew around the world — and then by small plane up to the forests of northern Malaysia, and then flew back, all in the space of eight days. It was a long and exhausting trip. This salad for two was meant to welcome her home with a taste of home and fresh greens. This was a very good salad — best ever, Carolyn said. But later I thought it would be even better with a little goat cheese added. It is very good that way, too.

1 bunch spinach
Olive oil
1/4 pound shiitake mushroom
    caps, sliced about
    1/4-inch thin
1/4 cup raw pine nuts
2 medium-sized Bosc pears
Balsamic vinaigrette
Goat cheese, optional

Serves 2 to 3

Cover the bottom of a flat salad bowl with freshly washed spinach leaves. Warm the olive oil in medium pan. Add sliced mushrooms and sauté until golden brown. Push mushrooms to side of pan, sprinkle in pine nuts and toast lightly (be careful not to burn them). Remove mushrooms and pine nuts from the pan and set aside.

Wash, halve, core, and slice pears. Place pears slices in pan and warm through on low for a couple of minutes. Pour balsamic vinaigrette over pears. Return shiitakes and pine nuts to pan, cover pan to warm through again. Arrange this mixture atop the spinach leaves.

Add the optional goat cheese.

Wisconsin-style Beer Batter Fish

Carol Van Dam, **Newscaster**

Nearly everyone I know in Wisconsin goes out to a Friday night fish fry at least twice a month. You usually get a choice of walleye pike, fresh lake trout (not corn fed), or cod filet — beer batter fish (fried or broiled) — all you can eat. It's a big part of the reason my family goes back to Milwaukee every summer.

BATTER: Blend and sift together flour, baking powder, and salt. Make a well in the center and pour in the oil, beer, and hot sauce. Stir together until ingredients are blended and smooth.

FISH: Heat oil in a pan or skillet until very hot. Dip fish pieces into the batter until covered and carefully drop into the hot oil. The oil should not cover the fish. Turn when browned on one side and brown on the other. Dip and fry all fish pieces until cooked (add oil as needed) and place on paper towels to drain.

Batter

1 cup flour
1 teaspoon baking powder
1-1/2 teaspoons salt
1 tablespoon oil
1 cup stale (no bubbles) beer
1/2 teaspoon hot sauce

Fish

Vegetable or other cooking oil
2 pounds fish, cut into pieces
    (cod filets work best)

Serves 4

Asides

Asides

Aloo Achaar (Indian Potato Salad)

Dorothy Hickson, **Transcript Coordinator**

I inherited this vegetarian recipe from my boyfriend's ex-roommate (it was originally on two very warped and splotchy pages from an old Madhur Jaffrey cookbook). Every year I make a double or triple batch to take along to the Philadelphia Folk Festival. My friends are all addicted. It's the perfect camp food because it just gets tastier after sitting around in a cooler for a day or two, marinating in its own spices.

Boil the potatoes. Combine sesame seeds, lemon juice, salt, and peppers in a stainless steel or non-metallic bowl. Whisk in the sesame oil, a few drops at a time.

Heat the vegetable oil in a metal ladle or butter warmer. When very hot, add fenugreek seeds. As soon as seeds begin to darken (this takes just a few seconds), pour the oil and spices into the dressing. Add parsley; mix well.

When the potatoes are cooked, drain and peel them. Dice into 3/4-inch cubes. Put potatoes in bowl with dressing and mix gently. Let cool, cover, and refrigerate.

4 medium potatoes
4 tablespoons ground roasted sesame seeds
3 tablespoons or more lemon juice
1 teaspoon salt
1 to 4 fresh hot jalapeño chilies, finely minced (or 2 tablespoons minced green pepper if you don't like things hot)
4 tablespoons sesame oil
2 teaspoons vegetable oil
8 to 10 whole fenugreek seeds
3 tablespoons fresh parsley

Serves 4

Austrian Palatschinken

Margot Adler, **NPR News Host/Correspondent**

My Dad was from Vienna. Most of our more interesting meals were Austrian, as is this recipe. My family was not really into cooking. My mother never learned to boil an egg until she was married. She tells a funny story about when my father was in the Army. She made him a lemon meringue pie using a recipe from a cookbook. She didn't realize you had to cook the meringue!

Pancake mix
Milk
1/4 teaspoon butter
6- to 9-inch cast iron skillet
    or frying pan
Jam

Make the pancake mix according to the directions on the box. Add milk until the batter is just a bit thicker than crepe batter, but much runnier than you would use to make regular pancakes. Melt butter in a 6- to 9-inch skillet. Using a ladle, put batter into the pan or skillet, enough to coat the bottom.

Brown the *palatschinken* on both sides, flip it into a warm plate, and fill the inside with your favorite jam. Black currant was my father's favorite, but try raspberry or strawberry. Carefully roll the pancake into a long tube (it should be about 1/2 to 3/4 of an inch round). Eat it as is, or sprinkle sugar on the top.

Basic Tomato Sauce

Lisa Simeone, **Host**

This is just a basic Italian tomato sauce recipe. I grew up eating it with slight variations by my grandmother that are not, alas, reproducible — believe me, we've tried. This sauce is very good, but it's not like my grandmother's. The first time I visited relatives in Italy — many years after my grandmother's death — I tasted a pasta-and-sauce dish, and I was transported back to my childhood.

In a large skillet or saucepan over low heat, add oil and sauté onions until they're translucent. While the onions are cooking, add as much garlic as you like. Add tomatoes and stir thoroughly. Add bay leaves and herbs to your taste. I sometimes add fennel seeds. In Sardinia, they add orange zest.

Cover and let simmer over low heat, stirring occasionally, until the tomatoes are soft and mushy, about 30 to 40 minutes. If the mixture gets too thick, you can add a little of the water you used to rinse out the final bits of tomato from the can.

2 onions, sliced
Olive oil, to your taste
3 cloves garlic, halved
1 28-ounce can whole
tomatoes
2 bay leaves
Various herbs
Orange zest, optional
Salt and pepper

Serves 4 to 5

Bialys

Bob Boilen, **NPR News Director**

I grew up in Brooklyn, N.Y., where bagels and bialys were a part of a weekend breakfast routine. I passed this tradition down to my son, Julian. Finding a good bagel in a different city is hard. Finding a bialy — impossible. When Julian began losing his front teeth, bagels were too hard so we decided to make bialys. We adapted this recipe and came up with something we could be proud to put our cream cheese on.

DOUGH: By bread machine: Add water and oil, then the flour, salt, and sugar. Make a well in the dry ingredients for the yeast (be sure the yeast doesn't touch anything except the flour). Put machine on dough cycle and prepare.

By hand: Combine the yeast, flour, sugar, salt, water, and oil and knead in the bowl with your hand for about 5 minutes.

TOPPING: Put water in a pan and bring to boil. Add onion. Cook for 2 to 3 minutes. Strain onions and discard water. Mix onions with the poppy seeds and oil and set aside.

Place dough on floured wax paper and sprinkle with flour. Flatten until it's less than 1 inch high. Using a 4-inch biscuit cutter, cut dough into rounds and place on a greased baking sheet. Use the bottom of a small juice glass to make a well in each round. Evenly fill each well with topping; let sit for 10 minutes. Bake at 375 degrees for 15 to 20 minutes; broil until crisp.

Dough
2 teaspoons active dry yeast
2-1/4 cups bread flour
1 tablespoon sugar
1 teaspoon kosher salt
1 tablespoon vegetable oil
1 cup water

Topping
2 cups water
1/2 cup chopped onion
2 tablespoons poppy seeds
1 tablespoon vegetable oil

Serves 4

Bloody Mary

Frank Deford, **Commentator**

H.L. Mencken said: "Never accept a drink during the day or turn one down at night." I think this is wise advice from the "sage of Baltimore," but the one exception I would make is to partake of a Bloody Mary at just the right daytime moment. Just one. A Bloody Mary may be delicious, but it is too filling to refill.

Pour as much vodka as interests you into a glass (the amount of vodka is optional — let your conscience be your guide). Adding the right amount of vodka isn't an exact science (this is not like making sure you use the right amount of baking powder).

Pour tomato juice in with the vodka as the base. Add a dash of Worcestershire sauce, a splash of lemon juice, a bit of pepper, and lots of ice. Under no circumstances should you use commercial Bloody Mary mix. That's for airplane drinking.

Stir with a celery stalk, for effect. As an alternative you could make a Bullshot, which is good in cold weather. Instead of tomato juice use beef bouillon or consommé, at 150 percent strength. All the other ingredients are the same.

Celery Seed Salad Dressing

Lucy Bremner, **Director, Special Development Projects**

Years ago, The English Tearoom on Boston's Newberry Street was a restaurant popular with graduate students who wanted to take a date or spouse for dinner "someplace nice" without breaking the bank. One of our fondest memories of meals there was the sweet and sour salad dressing. Later I tried Celery Seed Fruit Salad Dressing from a cookbook by the Women's Athletic Club in Chicago. I was amazed to find it tasted like the very dressing we loved in Boston. With some slight modifications, it has become a Bremner kitchen staple.

1 cup canola oil
1/2 cup granulated sugar
1/4 small onion, chopped
1 teaspoon Dijon mustard
1 teaspoon salt
1/2 cup cider vinegar
2 tablespoons whole celery seeds

Makes approximately 1-3/4 cups

Combine oil, sugar, onion, mustard, and salt in blender until sugar is dissolved. Add vinegar and celery seeds and blend until thoroughly combined. Store in refrigerator.

This is delicious on a salad made of romaine leaves, sliced banana, Belgian endive leaves, and sliced raw mushrooms. It's equally good on a salad of baby spinach leaves, thinly sliced red onion, canned mandarin oranges, and toasted pecan halves. If you are really trying to impress someone, substitute thinly sliced kumquats (skin on) for the mandarin oranges.

Chris' Holiday Brussels Sprouts

Chris Arnold, **Reporter**

I was told this recipe by a farmer who grew and sold Brussels sprouts at a market in San Francisco and I've been cooking them ever since. You may get to watch people look at the dish and say with some concern, "Oh, how unusual." Then you get to watch them eat their words and then eat your Brussels sprouts because they're sooo good.

2 to 3 pounds Brussels sprouts
3 tablespoons olive oil
3 to 5 cloves garlic, chopped, to taste
Oyster sauce

Serves 6

Wash and prep the Brussels sprouts. Trim a bit off the bottom of the stalks and pick off any outside leaves that look bad. Chop them in half (leave the little ones whole). Heat the oil in a wok or deep frying pan. Toss in the garlic and sauté for about 30 seconds. Add the Brussels sprouts.

Keep stirring until the sprouts start to get browned in spots. Add more oil if they start to stick to the pan as they brown.

Pour in the oyster sauce, thin with water to taste, and stir the mixture together. The first time you cook this, don't use a lot of oyster sauce. I've never really measured the amount, but you want the sprouts to have sauce on them, but not to be drowning in it.

Cover and steam the sprouts in the sauce for 10 minutes or until they're bright green and tender. Cook until they're soft enough to chew but not overcooked.

Cod: A Recipe for Disaster

Robin Hilton, **Associate Producer**

I only made this once, when I was 12 years old. It was a real showstopper. Only attempt this after your mother (or primary chef) leaves for the weekend. Wait for your father (or secondary chef) to suggest ordering in a pizza, then insist you can make a real dinner for everyone, all by yourself.

1 pound frozen cod filets
10-ounce package frozen peas
Plastic containers, assorted
    sizes
One large pot

Serves you right!

Preheat oven to 450 degrees. Set large pot of water (disproportionate to the actual amount of peas) on high to boil. Remove peas and cod from freezer. Bang lump of frozen cod against the counter to separate filets. Give up. Place frozen lump of cod on a cookie sheet, sprinkle with flour and set aside.

Watch television.

At the sound of the smoke alarm, run into kitchen. Notice smoke billowing from behind the oven door. Open to reveal large, flaming mass of melted plastic storage containers which primary chef stored in the oven without telling anyone. These will be a deep, crusty black and smell like burning tires.

The large pot of water should be boiling over by now. Remove from heat and set directly on the countertop while tending to oven fire. Open windows, flap arms, turn on fans, etc. Notice the smell from the pot of boiling water. Lift it up from countertop. A large glob of the counter will come up with it (it will resemble long, stringy, plastic cheese). Slosh some of the boiled water into the oven to douse the flames. Shut oven door. Cry to avoid a beating. Enjoy your pizza.

Curried Collards with Balsamic Vinegar

Dale Neiburg, **Technician, Satellite Operations**

I thought about inventing an exotic story about this recipe. My favorite was the one about how my great-great-grandfather, who served in the Swedish army under Charles XII, brought it back from the Crimea where he was given it in gratitude for having rescued the village chief's beautiful daughter. But the fact is, my wife improvised it from odds and ends that we happened to have around the house. It's an example of the creative value of improvisation and leftovers!

2 15-ounce cans collard greens
2 medium onions, chopped
2 tablespoons olive oil
1 teaspoon crushed red pepper flakes
2 tablespoons curry powder
1/2 cup balsamic vinegar

Serves 4

Drain and reserve liquid from collard greens. In a heavy 8-inch skillet, sauté onions in olive oil with the red pepper flakes and half the curry powder. Add the drained collards and sauté until almost dry. Add in 1 cup of reserved collard liquid, the balsamic vinegar, and the remaining curry powder. Simmer until liquid is almost gone.

Garlic Grits

Ann Taylor, **Newscaster**

Mother was a terrific cook. Unfortunately, I am not. This recipe was a favorite of mine, from a time before we started cutting down on butter. This is a southern dish — very rich and tasty — and may sway those who say they don't like grits.

Preheat oven to 350 degrees. Pour grits slowly into boiling salted water and cook until done, about 30 minutes. Cool slightly.

Melt butter and cheese (less 1 tablespoon). Stir in garlic. Add the butter and garlic mixture to the cooked grits. Beat eggs with milk, add cayenne pepper, and slowly stir into grits. Pour mixture into greased baking dish. Top with remaining cheese and cornflakes. Bake for 45 minutes.

4-1/2 cups water
1 cup grits
1 teaspoon salt
1/2 pound butter
1 cup shredded cheese
(or 1 roll garlic cheese)
3 cloves garlic, minced
2 eggs
1/2 cup milk
Pinch cayenne pepper
1 cup cornflakes

Serves 8

A Good Cup of Tea

Snigdha Prakash, **Reporter**

I like to start my day with a good cup of tea. It gives me a chance to savor the quiet before the day begins. Of course, I come from a nation of tea drinkers. Indians drink tea morning, noon, and night.

I'm picky about my tea. It has to be hot. It has to be strong. It has to have just the right amount of sugar — enough to bring out the taste of the tea, but not so much that it overpowers it. And it should have a little milk, NOT cream. Making good tea is easy. Just don't rush it.

Water
1 heaping teaspoon loose tea
(use the best you can find –
Assam, Ceylon, or a good
Irish or English breakfast
blend)
Sugar
Milk

Serves 1

Set water to boil. Add a heaping teaspoon of tea to a mug, preferably a china or ceramic mug.

Putter as the water comes to a boil — empty the dishwasher, gaze into the neighbor's yard, write a grocery list. Pour boiling water into the mug. Cover mug and let tea steep for 3 to 5 minutes.

Put your feet up while tea steeps.

Add a touch of milk and sugar to taste. Go back to your easy chair and enjoy your tea.

Repeat at least once or twice a day. Better still, do what I do. Coax your spouse or partner to make it for you. If you're lucky, they'll learn to make a better cup of tea than you do.

Herbal Crust-Free Quiche

Bruce Melzer, **Director, Online Business Development**

This is my wife Robyn Urbach's variation on the classic quiche recipe. She says, "If you are wheat intolerant, use rice or spelt flour. If you are dairy intolerant, add soy or rice cheese. If you can't remember what you're sensitive to, definitely use rosemary in this quiche — it's the herb that enhances memory."

6 eggs
1-1/2 cups milk
1/3 cup flour
1/4 teaspoon salt
1/4 teaspoon dry mustard
3/4 cup grated goat Gouda cheese
3/4 cup grated Armenian string cheese
Fresh sage
1 tablespoon butter

Serves 4 to 6

Preheat oven to 375 degrees. Grease a 9-inch pie plate with butter. Combine eggs, milk, flour, salt, mustard and mix well. Pour into pie plate. Sprinkle cheese on top of the quiche. Sauté small fresh sage leaves in butter until crisp and sprinkle over the top of the egg and cheese mixture. Bake for 45 minutes or until the middle is set and the quiche puffs a bit.

You can substitute 1 teaspoon dried thyme, 1 1/2 teaspoons dried rosemary, or 1 teaspoon dried oregano. If you use all 3, cut amounts by 1/3.

Hunting & Gathering

Richard Harris, **Correspondent**

The truth is, you don't need to be an accomplished cook to absorb plenty of calories at NPR. The building is full of hidden stashes. Peggy Girshman is the most popular person on the third floor — and people swear it's not simply because she has a file cabinet full of old Halloween (or new Easter) candy. *Morning Edition* has a 7 a.m. doughnut run by a producer mysteriously known as the Bad Melissa. Joanne Silberner has two — yes, two — drawers full of chocolate.

Birthday cakes commonly crop up on community tables. The best way to find them is to follow Jon "Smokey" Baer around — his nose puts real bear olfaction to shame. Folks in *Performance Today*® are always happy when Fred Child's girlfriend is in town, because that means homemade cookies for them.

Food often appears in random places after people have been on trips. Salt water taffy is always a hit. The hungry mob even managed to gobble up dried cuttlefish from Southeast Asia. About the only food that languished was a paper bag of *dulse,* carried lovingly from Nova Scotia. It turns out *dulse* is red seaweed. Sandy red seaweed.

After holidays, people find themselves burdened with comestibles that have the caloric equivalent of high explosives. There's only one way to dispose safely of material like that. Give it to the science desk. We have the technology (a knife in the supply cabinet) and the stomachs to get the job done.

Irish Raisin Bread

Pam Fessler, **Correspondent**

This is from my grandmother, Elizabeth Dunn, who emigrated from Tullamore, Ireland, to New York in 1904 at the age of 20. She used to make this bread every time she visited us at our home in New Jersey. I have especially fond memories of coming home after midnight Mass on Christmas Eve and eating a nice slice of raisin bread with butter before going to sleep. Today, this bread remains a family treat.

4 cups flour
4 teaspoons baking powder
1 teaspoon salt
3/4 cup sugar
2 cups raisins
2 tablespoons butter
1-1/2 cups milk

Serves 6

Preheat oven to 350 degrees. Combine the flour, baking powder, salt, and sugar. Mix in the raisins until completely coated. Melt the butter in the pan you plan to cook the bread in. (In my house we always used a 10-inch cast iron skillet, but I've also cooked it in a 10-inch pie plate.) Make sure the butter coats the bottom of the pan. Drain the extra butter into the dry ingredients and stir.

Slowly pour milk into dry mixture, stirring until it is stiff and doughy (I add a tablespoon or two of milk if it seems too dry). Put the dough in the buttered pan, shaping it into a round loaf. Bake for 45 minutes to 1 hour. Bread should be a golden brown. Cool for about an hour and remove from pan. Slice when completely cooled.

Jalapeño Jelly

Renee Montagne, **NPR News Host**

Everyone called my grandmother "Mama" in a tone that was one part respect, two parts love, and a heaping tablespoon of awe. Mama cooked on a black, cast iron, wood-burning stove decades past the day electricity arrived at their homestead in the wild sand hills of Nebraska. How modern my mother and my aunt Alyce must have felt in their own 1950s kitchens. Among the exotic recipes they experimented with that became family classics was my aunt Alyce's bright green jalapeño jelly. I found a smudged card in her little recipe box, and offer it below.

1/2 cup jalapeño peppers
3/4 cup green peppers
6 cups sugar
1-1/2 cups cider vinegar
6 ounces pectin
8 drops green food coloring
Cheesecloth
6 half-pint jelly jars

Serves many

Sterilize the jars just before you start cooking the jelly so the jars remain hot. Remove seeds from jalapeño and green peppers. Mix in blender until smooth. In large heavy saucepan, mix peppers, sugar, and vinegar and bring to boil. Boil one minute, and then remove from heat.

Cool slightly, then add pectin and food coloring. Stir until blended, and then quickly strain the jelly through cheesecloth, using a large spoon to push it through, into hot sterilized jars. Seal. Once the jars are open, refrigerate.

This is delicious on crackers with cream cheese.

John's Tex/New Mex Barbecue Rub

John Burnett, **Correspondent**

"I don't cook!" I told my wife, Ginny, who is a genius in the kitchen. "What can I submit for the NPR cookbook?" "You smoke meat," she replied. "Barbecuing is cooking." She always has the right answer. So here it is, my recipe for John's Tex/New Mex Barbecue Rub.

A rub is a concoction of spices applied to meat prior to barbecuing. I literally rub the spices into the raw meat and refrigerate it an hour before cooking. By barbecue, I mean meat that is cooked — grilled, broiled or, preferably, smoked — over open coals, the slower the better. I own an indirect smoking pit, in which the fire is kept off to one side and the meat is cooked by indirect heat and infused by smoke from seasoned oak, pecan, or mesquite that I keep in separate piles in my backyard.

I prefer the taste of a rub to that of a mop sauce, or basting sauce, which is a lot of trouble to continually apply during a three-hour smoking session. (Every time you open the pit to mop the meat you let out the heat!)

2 tablespoons coarse sea salt

2 tablespoons coarse ground pepper

1 tablespoon ground red chili pepper, preferably from Chimayo, N.M.

2 teaspoons garlic powder

Burns a few

Mix ingredients thoroughly and rub into meat. I find this works best on pork tenderloin, pork ribs, beef brisket, and any good steak. Beware — it's spicy.

Kasha Varnishkes

Ketzel Levine, **Senior Correspondent**

My mother, Rosalind Kopman Levine, got this recipe from her mother, Nancy Steinberg Kopman, when she was growing up in Brooklyn, N.Y. She typically made kasha varnishkes to go with pot roast and gravy. As a lifelong vegetarian, I've grown to love it all on its own.

1 large onion, diced
1 box bowtie-shaped pasta
    (farfalle)
1 cup buckwheat groats
    (kasha)
1 egg, beaten
2 cups hot water
Vegetable oil or butter
Salt and pepper

Serves 4 to 6

Sauté onion in oil or butter until slightly browned. Set aside. Cook pasta until it's just done but not soft (*al dente*). Remove from heat, drain, and set aside.

While heating a 10-ounce pan, put beaten egg into kasha and mix thoroughly. Put kasha and egg mixture into the heated pan and swirl around until blended, but do not allow it to stick or burn.

When kasha is cooked completely dry, pour water over it and mix well. Set on a low flame; water will be absorbed. Remove from heat. Mix onions, pasta, and kasha together. Salt and pepper to taste.

Mama Stamberg's Cranberry Relish

Susan Stamberg, **Special Correspondent**

I'm happy to share my late mother-in-law Marjorie Stamberg's Thanksgiving recipe. My family and I hope you enjoy it, and that it will become a tradition in your household. And remember, it's the recipe that sounds terrible, but tastes terrific! The tangy taste cuts through and perks up the turkey and gravy. It's also good on next-day turkey sandwiches, and with roast beef.

2 cups whole raw cranberries
1 small onion
3/4 cup sour cream
1/2 cup sugar
2 tablespoons horseradish
(the red is milder than
the white)

Makes 1-1/2 pints

Grind the raw berries and onion together. (I use an old-fashioned meat grinder. If you use a food processor, you want to end up with a chunky grind, not a purée.) Mix in sour cream, sugar, and horseradish. Put in a plastic container and freeze.

Early Thanksgiving morning, move it from freezer to refrigerator compartment to thaw (it should still have some little icy slivers left). The relish will be thick, creamy, and shocking pink.

Mashed Potatoes with Garlic & Olive Oil

Patrick Murray, **Broadcast/Recording Technician**

When I joined NPR, this recipe became my contribution to the Thanksgiving potluck dinner for those who have to work that day. When I left for the West Coast, much e-mail went back and forth to assure that this recipe would continue to be part of the Thanksgiving tradition at NPR. It's adapted from Sarah Leah Chase's *Cold-Weather Cooking*. This feeds a crowd — cut ingredient amounts to suit the number of guests.

15 pounds medium-sized red skinned potatoes
30 large cloves garlic, unpeeled
2-1/2 to 3 cups extra virgin olive oil
Kosher salt and freshly ground pepper to taste

Serves 25 to 30 staff

Place potatoes and garlic cloves in a large pot with enough water to cover by at least an inch, with space enough for what I call "boiling room." (Wrap the garlic in cheesecloth for ease in fishing out later.) Bring to a boil over high heat. Reduce to a simmer and cook uncovered until the potatoes are tender.

Drain the potatoes and garlic. Set the garlic aside. Return the potatoes to the pot in small batches, and cook over medium heat for 1 to 2 minutes to evaporate the excess liquid. Place the potatoes back in the pot. Squeeze the garlic pulp from the skins and add to the potatoes.

Beat the potatoes with a hand mixer until fluffy. With the mixer running slowly, beat in 2 cups of olive oil. Save the rest for later. Rush the pot to NPR by noon so the potatoes are still hot and mix in the rest of the oil. Add the salt and pepper to taste.

Mint Julep

Bob Edwards, **NPR News Host**

Pour straight Kentucky sour mash bourbon over ice in a sturdy glass. Think about rows of mint in a garden. Think about the mint left on your pillow in a comfortable hotel room at the end of a long day on the road. Think about the United States Mint churning out coins that are used to actually buy things. Think about any kind of mint you like, but don't let any of it get near the glass.

What you are holding is not a mint julep, but rather a bourbon on the rocks, a much more satisfying refreshment than some girly drink with too much sugar and some ugly leaves in it. While enjoying the bourbon, play a Ray Charles CD that includes his early '60s instrumental hit, "One Mint Julep." Turn up the volume.

Refill glass as desired. Smoke 'em if you got 'em.

Bourbon
Ice

Serves 1

Persian Lemons

Jacki Lyden, **Alternate Weekend Host**

I love Persian lemons, a fancy name given to the pickled lemons I learned to love in Iran. In Iran they are actually sweet lemons, something I think you can buy in a California market. Since no one I know here in New York has sweet lemons on hand for pickling, I use plain old lemons. Pickled lemons are an ancient treat, they look beautiful in your refrigerator, and there are hundreds of ways to use them. They can be added to almost anything, cold or hot. I use them when I make homemade chicken soup, but I really like them best in a cold white bean salad. I make sautéed chicken with preserved lemon, and I also add them to sautéed spinach, salad dressings, and regular salad. They are sort of sweet-sour; I think anyone who likes pickles or olives will love them!

1-quart jar or any jar with
    a tight lid
6 lemons (more if they fit)
Kosher salt
Lemon juice

Cut the lemons in half, but not all the way in half, and then slice them lengthwise, but not all the way lengthwise (they should still be connected by the skin but have two deep slits in them).

Pack the slits with coarse kosher salt (this is a larger grain than regular salt). Cram your lemons into the quart jar and add another cup of salt (I'd say about a cup of extra salt per half dozen of lemons).

Cover with lemon juice and let stand in your refrigerator for 6 weeks. They look beautifully sunny during a drab winter, and beautifully sparkly in the hot summer.

Rainbow Potato Salad

Fredessa Hamilton, **Manager, Technology Training**

This is a really simple recipe, but it makes a very beautiful presentation when it's done. I serve this year-round, but it's especially pretty during the winter holiday season. The original potato salad recipe was my mom's and grandmother's, but I added the variety of peppers — I'm into colors!

5 pounds white potatoes
2 hard-boiled eggs
1 large onion
1/2 green pepper
1/2 red pepper
1/2 orange pepper
1/2 purple pepper, optional
1 cup chopped celery
1 tablespoon pimento
1 tablespoon sweet relish
1 teaspoon mustard
1 cup mayonnaise
Salt and pepper
Paprika

Serves 6 to 8 people

You'll need a really big mixing bowl and a big sturdy cooking spoon.

Boil potatoes, skin on, until they're softened but not mushy. Drain, rinse with cold water, and peel. Slice potatoes into cubes. Peel and dice the hard-boiled eggs. Chop, mince or cube onion, peppers, and celery.

Combine all these ingredients in a very large mixing bowl, along with the pimento, relish, mustard, and mayonnaise. Add a little more mayonnaise if potato salad is really hard to stir (but not so much as to make it mashed potato salad!).

Add salt and pepper to taste. Finish with a sprinkling of paprika on top.

Raspberry Shrub

Mara Riley, **Traffic Manager, Corporate Sponsorship**

"Shrub" is a refreshing 18th-century hot weather drink that can be made in a number of different ways. This is my favorite, which I bring to 18th-century reenactment events. The mixture of vinegar and sugar may seem odd, but the vinegar cuts the sugar and keeps it from being too cloying.

1 quart white vinegar
1 quart frozen raspberries, blueberries, or blackberries
4 cups sugar or equivalent amount of syrup

Put the berries in a large glass jar. Pour the vinegar over the berries. Put a lid on the jar and let steep, on a sunny windowsill if possible, anywhere from overnight to several days. Strain. To the flavored vinegar, add the sugar or syrup. If using sugar, simmer and stir until the sugar dissolves. If using syrup, it's about 1 tablespoon of syrup to one glass of water, or to taste.

To serve with wine, mix 1 part shrub to 2 parts white wine. Chill and serve. Some people like this with seltzer, ginger ale, or champagne, or poured over vanilla ice cream.

Tuna Fish Pasta Sauce

Joe Palca, **Correspondent**

This recipe is adapted from *The Classic Cooking of the Italian Jews* by Edda Servi Machlin. My first reaction when I saw the recipe was, "Yuk. Tuna and tomatoes? No way." But a friend coaxed me into trying it, and it was excellent. It's one of those recipes you get to play around with. Add more or less oil, more or less parsley, more or less garlic. Real aficionados prefer tuna packed in olive oil, found in gourmet stores.

Heat oil and red pepper flakes over medium-high flame in a 12-inch skillet. When oil is hot, add parsley. Reduce heat and sauté parsley for about 5 minutes. Add tomato paste and tuna. Stir for about 1 minute.

Add garlic, tomatoes, and red wine. Bring to boil, then reduce heat and simmer for 10 minutes. Serve over pasta. Garnish with fresh parsley.

1/4 cup olive oil

1/4 teaspoon red pepper flakes (more if you can take it, less if you can't)

1-1/2 cups chopped fresh parsley (save some for garnish)

2 tablespoons tomato paste

1 6-ounce can tuna in water or oil, drained

1 clove garlic, minced

1 15-ounce can chopped tomatoes

1 cup dry red wine

Serves 4

Vine-fresh Tomato Sauce

Howard Berkes, **Correspondent**

In my role covering rural affairs, I pass a lot of roadside stands teeming with fresh vegetables. Tomato season brings out this favorite dish. It's based on a recipe that first appeared in *The Catalyst,* a Salt Lake City magazine and is reprinted by permission. I consider this a colorful and savory alternative to conventional pasta sauces, especially for summer dinners *al fresco*.

Heat the olive oil to sizzling. Sauté the garlic, onion, zucchini, and pepper until limp and just turning color. Stir the basil and white wine into the sautéed vegetables and heat. Add the tomatoes and cook, stirring, just until they're heated through.

The original recipe calls for boiling or singeing the tomatoes, and then peeling them. I don't bother. Serve over pasta, sprinkled with cheese and parsley.

2 tablespoons olive oil
2 cloves garlic, minced
1 medium onion or 8 scallions, chopped with green tops
1 small zucchini, finely chopped
1 red bell pepper, chopped
2 tablespoons fresh basil, minced
1/4 cup dry white wine
4 large freshly picked tomatoes, chopped
1/2 cup freshly grated Parmesan cheese
Minced parsley for garnish

Serves 4

Zucchini Bread

Tiffany Coe, **Contracts Manager**

My mom has been making this recipe for as long as I can remember. When my parents lived in California, their first gardening experience yielded an overly abundant crop of zucchini. A neighbor passed along this recipe, which offers a unique way to use a lot of zucchini. It's been a popular treat in my family — it's tasty with cream cheese or by itself. Even people who are typically anti-zucchini seem to like it.

Preheat oven to 350 degrees. Beat eggs with mixer. Continue beating while adding sugar, then oil, and grated zucchini. In a small bowl, mix together flour, baking soda, baking powder, salt, and cinnamon.

In mixer, on low speed, add flour mixture to zucchini mixture. Add vanilla. Stir in chopped prunes and optional nuts. Pour into two greased and floured 5 x 9-inch loaf pans or three smaller pans, stirring batter right before pouring. Bake for 55 to 60 minutes. Test with toothpick. Cool in pans 15 minutes before transferring to wire rack.

3 eggs
1 cup granulated sugar
1 cup packed dark brown sugar
3/4 cup oil
2 cups grated zucchini
2 cups sifted flour
2 teaspoons baking soda
1/4 teaspoon baking powder
1/4 teaspoon salt
1 tablespoon cinnamon
1 tablespoon vanilla
1 cup chopped prunes
1/2 cup chopped nuts, if desired

Serves 4 to 6

Sweet Endings

Sweet Endings

Aunt Hermina's Apple Cake

Peter Breslow, **Supervising Senior Producer**

This recipe comes from my Aunt Hermina. She was Hungarian, high-strung, and lived in Passaic, N.J. Aunt Hermina was also a wonderful cook. I've never made this cake, but my wife has, and I like to eat it. It's great to serve for brunch or dessert.

Preheat oven to 350 degrees. Grease a 9-inch tube pan. Combine sliced apples with 5 tablespoons of sugar and the cinnamon and set aside. Sift flour and remaining sugar and place in large bowl. Add baking powder and salt. Make a well in center. Pour in oil, eggs, juice, and vanilla. Mix by hand.

Spoon 1/3 of the batter into tube pan. Drain the liquid from the apple mixture. Place ring of apples over mixture. Add some raisins and nuts if desired. Spoon another 1/3 of batter over this. Add remaining apples, nuts, and raisins. Top with the remaining 1/3 batter. Bake for approximately 90 minutes. Cover the top with foil if cake gets too brown. Cool until lukewarm before removing from pan.

5 apples, sliced (about 3 cups)
5 tablespoons plus 2 cups of sugar
5 teaspoons cinnamon
3 cups flour
3 teaspoons baking powder
1 teaspoon salt
1 cup oil
4 eggs
1/4 cup orange juice
1 tablespoon vanilla
Raisins, walnuts, or pecans, optional

Serves 4 to 6

Auntie's Tollhouse Chocolate Sauce

Peter Overby, **Correspondent**

**This was my wife's Aunt Flo's special "company" dessert, and now it's
ours, too. The source of this recipe, unfortunately, is lost in the mists
of time. Auntie Flo was a public school teacher and principal in Jersey
City, N.J. She never married, toured the world with her friends, took
her sherry in a cut-crystal glass, and lived to be 100.**

Melt butter. Add chopped chocolate. Stir over low heat until it melts together.
Add sugar, cream, salt, vanilla, and cocoa. Bring to boiling, and then remove
from flame. Chill. This keeps in the refrigerator for a long, long time. Gently
reheat as needed and serve over vanilla ice cream or pound cake.

1/4 cup butter

2 ounces unsweetened baking
chocolate

3/4 cup sugar

1/2 cup light cream or half
and half

Salt

1 teaspoon vanilla

1/4 cup unsweetened cocoa
powder

Carrot Cake for a Crowd

Julie Rovner, **Correspondent**

This is my favorite birthday cake and the only dessert I like better than chocolate anything. This is adapted from the *Better Homes and Gardens All-Time Favorite Recipes,* with alterations inspired by my vegetarian college roommate.

CAKE: Preheat oven to 325 degrees. Stir together flour, sugar, baking powder, baking soda, cinnamon, and salt. Add carrot, pineapple, oil, eggs, and 1/4 cup of the nuts. Mix until moistened, then beat at medium speed for 2 minutes. Pour into greased and floured 13 x 9 x 2-inch pan and bake for 50 to 60 minutes. Let cool at least an hour; do not cover while warm or the top will get sticky.

FROSTING: For the frosting, beat the cream cheese and butter until fluffy. Slowly add in the confectioners' sugar until the mixture is smooth. Stir in vanilla. Frost cake when it is fully cooled and top with the remaining nuts.

Cake

2 cups all-purpose flour
2 cups granulated sugar
1 teaspoon baking powder
1 teaspoon baking soda
1 teaspoon ground cinnamon
1 teaspoon salt
2-1/2 cups shredded carrot
1/2 cup crushed pineapple
1 cup cooking oil
4 eggs
1/2 cup chopped walnuts

Frosting

1 3-ounce package cream cheese, softened at room temperature
1/4 cup butter
2 cups confectioners' sugar
1 teaspoon vanilla

Serves 6 to 8

Chocolate Chip Cookies

Ellen Weiss, **Senior National Editor**

Baking cookies serves a couple of purposes in my life — it helps me relax, it's something my boys love to do with me, and it helps break the tension at work. I originally got my recipe from the back of the bag of semisweet chocolate chips. It's still the best. I believe the secret to good cookies is in the softness of the margarine (I never use butter) and the number of small children's fingers in the batter.

2-1/4 cups of flour
1 teaspoon baking soda
2 eggs
2 sticks margarine, softened
3/4 cup brown sugar
3/4 cup granulated sugar
1 teaspoon vanilla
2 cups chocolate chips
Nuts, optional

Preheat oven to 350 degrees. Combine flour and baking soda.

In a separate bowl, beat 2 eggs. Blend in margarine, sugar, and vanilla. Add flour mixture slowly and beat with an electric mixer until creamy.

Stir in two cups chocolate chips and nuts, if desired. Drop rounded teaspoons of batter onto an ungreased cookie sheet. Bake for 10 to 12 minutes or until golden. Remove from oven and cool on rack.

Cowboy Cookies

Melissa Gray, **Associate Producer**

These cookies became a Christmas staple in 1988. My mom and I bake about seven different types of cookies to share with friends and family. We usually buy nuts, chips, and raisins in bulk, but somehow we never manage to finish up that last handful. Not anymore.

The great thing about this recipe is that you can create your own combinations: chocolate chip and peanut butter chips; dried cherries and butterscotch (my favorite); or white chocolate chips and nuts. Don't overdo the chunky stuff or the batter will get way too crumbly.

1 cup granulated sugar
1 cup brown sugar
1 cup shortening
2 eggs, beaten
2 cups flour
1 teaspoon soda
1 teaspoon salt
2 cups oats
1 teaspoon vanilla

Preheat oven to 350 degrees. Blend sugars and shortening. Add eggs. Add flour, soda, and salt. Stir in oats. Add vanilla. Mix, then add chocolate chips, peanut butter chips, raisins, nuts, whatever chunky cookie-type ingredients you want. Drop by teaspoonful onto baking sheet. Bake for 10 minutes.

Dave's "Cart Cake" & Orange Glaze

Lynn Neary, **Correspondent/Host**

Not long after I met my husband, he invited me to dinner at his home. During dinner he told me we were having "cart" cake for dessert. I had no idea what that was, but since the dinner was so good I figured dessert would be, too. When he finally served it, I was surprised to find out it was actually carrot cake. My husband's Canadian accent had turned it into "cart" cake to my ear! It was, and still is, the best carrot cake I have ever eaten, so I like to think of it as the cake that won my heart.

CAKE: Preheat oven to 325 degrees. Beat eggs. Add sugar and oil and mix until blended. Sift dry ingredients together in a separate bowl. Blend into egg mixture slowly. Fold in carrots and nuts. Pour into a greased and floured 8- or 9-inch springform pan or tube pan. Bake for 60 minutes or until center springs back when touched. Remove from oven when done and let cool in the pan before removing. Glaze when cooled.

GLAZE: Zest and juice a large orange. In a small saucepan, cook sugar and orange juice over medium heat until syrupy. Add zest and drizzle over cooled cake.

Cake
2 eggs
1 cup granulated sugar
3/4 cup vegetable oil
1 cup flour
1/2 teaspoon salt
1 teaspoon baking soda
1 teaspoon cinnamon
1/4 teaspoon nutmeg
1/4 teaspoon allspice
1-1/2 cups grated carrots
1/2 cup chopped nuts or raisins, optional

Orange Glaze
1 large orange
1/4 cup sugar

Serves 6 to 8

Dewberry Cobbler

JC Patrick, **Station Development Manager**

**After a big barbecue dinner, you have to have something sweet.
Dewberries are a kind of wild blackberry. In Texas, you know the
dewberries are ripe when the snakes and turtles have purple mouths!**

**If you don't feel like strolling along the side of the railroad tracks
with a large stick and a pail, grabbing dewberries before the wild
things do — then blackberries, canned cherries, blueberries — any
kind of firm berry will suffice.**

3 cups berries
3 cups sugar
1 cup plus 2 tablespoons flour
1/4 cup butter
3/4 cup milk
2 teaspoons baking powder
1/2 teaspoon salt

Serves 4

Preheat oven to 350 degrees. Wash and drain berries. Pour 2 cups sugar
over berries, and let sit to sweeten. Sprinkle with 2 tablespoons of flour.
Melt butter in baking dish (a small round casserole is good for this cobbler).

Sift flour and remaining 1 cup sugar. Add to the butter. Add milk, baking
powder, and salt. Mix well. Pour berries over batter. Do not mix together.
Bake for 45 minutes.

Edith's Gingerbread

Melissa Block, **NPR News Host**

I'm a huge fan of gingerbread. It's comforting and not too sweet. You can almost convince yourself it's good for you. This recipe is from one of my favorite writers about food and eating and the pleasures of travel, M.F.K. Fisher. It's her mother's recipe and is included in her 1942 book *How to Cook a Wolf.* **It sends out a fine, friendly smell through the house. A nice mound of whipped cream on top doesn't hurt.**

Preheat oven to 325 degrees. Sift together the flour, baking powder, cinnamon, ginger, cloves, and salt. In a separate bowl, combine the butter and sugar until the mixture is very well mixed.

Beat 1/2 teaspoon baking soda into the molasses and mix well. Add to the butter and sugar. Mix the remaining 1/4 teaspoon baking soda into 3/4 cup boiling water and stir. Alternate adding this and the sifted dry ingredients to the butter mixture. Fold in the egg and pour into a greased and floured 8-inch square pan. The batter may seem too thin for a cake, but do not increase the quantity of flour as many doubting cooks have done.

Bake for 30 minutes or until a toothpick inserted in the middle comes out clean (I like to undercook it a little). Eat as is or top with whipped cream, ice cream or wine sauce.

1-1/4 cups flour
1 teaspoon baking powder
1 teaspoon cinnamon
1 teaspoon ginger
1 teaspoon ground cloves
1/2 teaspoon salt
1 cup butter
1/4 cup sugar
3/4 teaspoon baking soda
1/2 cup molasses
1 cup boiling water
1 egg, lightly beaten

Serves 4 to 6

Grandma Keator's Chocolate Cake

John Keator, **Director, Telecommunications**

This is the most popular recipe in the church cookbook at my mother's church in Maine. It's a simple, inexpensive cake, but it tastes rich and fudgy. It has been a favorite in the Keator family for four generations.

Preheat oven to 350 degrees. In small bowl, mix cocoa and coffee into a paste. Set aside. Combine shortening and sugar. Add egg and vanilla and beat well. Combine flour, baking soda, and salt.

Add combined dry ingredients alternately with buttermilk to shortening mixture. Stir in cocoa paste. Pour into greased and floured 8 x 8-inch pan (batter will be thin) and bake 40 to 45 minutes until cake tests done. Cake will be flat, not puffy. Frost as desired.

1/2 cup unsweetened cocoa
1/3 cup hot coffee
2 tablespoons shortening
1 cup sugar
1 egg
1 teaspoon vanilla
1 cup flour, sifted
1 teaspoon baking soda
1/2 teaspoon salt
3/4 cup buttermilk or sour milk

Serves 9

Harvey's Chocolate Mousse

Ira Flatow, **Host**

I was having a New Year's Eve party to celebrate the bicentennial and had asked everyone to bring a dish. I had everything prepared except a good, rich dessert. In a panic, I tagged my friend Harvey Smith, a Washington D.C. trial lawyer, whose secret weapon was a deadly chocolate mousse. The secret is that it's easy to make and sure to please even the most addicted chocoholic. ("Put it in my bowl and no one gets hurt.")

8 egg yolks
8 ounces superfine sugar
3 to 4 ounces chocolate-orange liqueur
1 pound semisweet chocolate
1 quart heavy cream

Serves 6 to 8

Beat egg yolks and sugar until light and creamy. Mix in liqueur.

Melt chocolate in a double boiler over hot water while whipping the cream. Mix a little cream into yolk mixture, then mix in chocolate until smooth. Fold in rest of whipped cream.

Dish out — and lick the bowl.

Impossible Pumpkin Pie

Julie McCarthy, **Correspondent**

The exact origin of this, the world's easiest dessert, is unknown, but it seems to have been first tested in my hometown of Kenosha, Wis. The *Impossible Pumpkin Pie* recipe was handed down 54 years ago to another daughter of Kenosha, 76-year-old Lois M. Kronholm. Her Aunt Gerda presented it to Lois at her bridal shower. Gerda Blaed was no ordinary aunt: she was the city's most celebrated caterer. "You didn't do a party without Mrs. Blaed," said Margaret Urban, a contemporary of Lois Kronholm, so the recipe would seem to have a "pedigree" of sorts. I have adjusted the ingredients to my taste. You want this light, smooth, and not overly spicy.

1/2 cup sugar

1/2 cup biscuit mix

2 tablespoons butter or margarine

1 13-ounce can evaporated milk

2 eggs

1 16-ounce can pumpkin

2 teaspoons pumpkin pie spice

1 teaspoon vanilla

Serves 4 to 6

Heat oven to 350 degrees. Grease a 9-inch pie pan. Beat all ingredients together until smooth, about 2 minutes, with electric mixer. When blended thoroughly, pour into pie pan. Bake 50 or 55 minutes. Serve with whipped cream.

Laura's Pound Cake

Michele Norris, **NPR News Host**

This has been in our family for generations. It is a very simple cake but very rich in flavor and something you can tart up easily with sautéed fruit, a caramel drizzle, powdered sugar stencils, or a dollop of whipped or ice cream. As for me, I like it plain, on a delicate dessert plate, accompanied by a strong cup of coffee. Good stuff.

1-1/2 teaspoons vanilla or
　　lemon extract
2/3 cup milk
1 pound butter
3 cups sugar
6 eggs
4 cups cake flour

Serves 6

Preheat oven to 350 degrees. Mix extract with milk and set aside. Cream butter and sugar until smooth. Add eggs, one at a time, beating after each addition.

Add flour, 2 cups at a time alternately with the milk mixture (begin and end with flour). Beat after each addition. I mean really beat it!

Put into greased and floured cake pan and bake for 1-1/2 hours. Insert a toothpick; if it comes out dry, the cake is done.

Lorentz Invariant Molasses Cake

David Kestenbaum, **Correspondent**

This is my grandmother's recipe. It has been tested against a placebo and shown to be very effective.

CAKE: Preheat oven to 325 degrees. Mix sugar and butter together until creamy. Add eggs, spices, molasses, and flour. Put baking soda into 1 cup boiling water, mix and add to the batter. Grease and flour a 13 x 9 inch pan. Add batter and bake for 40 minutes.

ICING: Cut chocolate into small pieces. Combine chocolate, sugar, butter, and milk in a saucepan. Boil for 1 or 2 minutes. Remove from heat and add vanilla. Ice cake only after it has cooled. Hide cake from friends and family.

Cake
1/2 cup sugar
1/2 cup butter
2 eggs
1 teaspoon cinnamon
1 teaspoon ground cloves
1 teaspoon ground ginger
3/4 cup molasses
2 cups cake flour
1 teaspoon baking soda (This is an important ingredient. Don't leave it out. My sister did.)
1 cup boiling water

Icing
3 squares unsweetened baking chocolate
1 cup sugar
1 rounded teaspoon butter
5 tablespoons milk
1 teaspoon vanilla

Serves 6

Martha Cake

Linda Wertheimer, **Senior Correspondent**

This recipe came to my mother from Martha Stewart. Not that Martha Stewart. Our Martha taught school with my aunt Hester Gault in Carlsbad, N.M. This cake was a great favorite in our family — not only is it easy to make, my mother thought it really shone as a dessert to take to church suppers or potluck dinners. Once it's baked and given a good soaking, it can go for miles in the trunk of a car and never feel a thing.

CAKE: Preheat oven to 350 degrees. Cream together the shortening, salt, sugar, and eggs. In a food processor, chop together raisins, orange peel, and pecans. Combine the two mixtures and mix well. Dissolve baking soda in buttermilk. Add to mixture, along with vanilla and flour. Mix quickly to combine. Pour into 9 x 9-inch square pan and bake for about 40 minutes (until a toothpick poked into the center comes out clean).

DRIZZLE: While the cake is baking, dissolve sugar in orange juice. Pour the sweetened juice evenly over the top of the cake immediately after baking. Poke a few holes in the cake to be sure it soaks in evenly. Serve directly from the baking pan. The first piece will be a mess (you'll have to eat that one). You might want to serve it with unsweetened whipped cream, or if you really must, vanilla ice cream. At Christmas or Thanksgiving, I sometimes substitute dried cranberries for raisins. The recipe can be doubled and baked in a roasting pan.

Cake
1/2 cup shortening
1 teaspoon salt
1 cup sugar
2 eggs
1 cup golden raisins soaked in
    water, then drained
1 orange (peel only)
1 cup pecans
1 teaspoon baking soda
1 cup buttermilk
1 teaspoon vanilla
2 cups flour

Drizzle
2/3 cup sugar
1/2 cup fresh orange juice

Serves 4 to 6

Molten Chocolate Bombs

Daniel Jacobson, **Programmer, NPR Online**

The fact that I work at NPR got me in the door with my fiancée, but when I served her my mom's Molten Chocolate Bombs, it sealed the deal. After all, nobody can resist an unforgettable dish that marries the essential qualities of a perfect dessert — chocolate and gooey-fudgy chocolate. And if you really want to enrich the experience, serve with white chocolate raspberry ice cream!

Preheat the oven to 400 degrees. Using additional butter at room temperature, grease the bottom and sides of six 6-ounce custard cups. Line the bottoms of the cups with parchment paper, then lightly butter paper and set aside.

Melt the chocolate in a double boiler or microwave oven. Set aside to cool slightly. Combine the butter, sugar, salt, and eggs. Beat until well blended. Gradually add the cake flour and mix well. Add the vanilla and cooled chocolate and blend until smooth.

Divide the batter evenly among the cups and smooth the surfaces with a small rubber spatula. Place cups on a baking sheet, and bake until the tops are well puffed, about 15 minutes. Cool for 5 minutes in cups, remove from cups, peel off parchment paper, and serve.

12 ounces finest quality bittersweet or semisweet chocolate, finely chopped
3 tablespoons unsalted butter, room temperature (plus additional butter for greasing pan)
2/3 cup granulated sugar
1/8 teaspoon salt
4 eggs, room temperature, lightly beaten
1/2 cup cake flour
1 teaspoon vanilla

Serves 6

Mom's Oven-sauce Chocolate Pudding

Jean Cochran, **Newscaster**

This dessert is a treasured memory of the 1950s for me. My mom would serve it for Sunday dinner or for guests. The recipe card indicates she got it from her mother, so I don't know how old it really is (Mom is 88). I've made it myself to great effect; it's actually very easy. Use whatever kind of chocolate you like, but I prefer dark. It comes out looking like brownies or cake, but there's a wonderful pudding sauce on the bottom — and you can spoon some on top of each serving. It's a wonderful chocolate mess. Serve warm or cold and top with whipped cream to be really decadent.

1/4 cup shortening
1/2 teaspoon salt
1 teaspoon cinnamon
1/4 cup sugar
3 1-ounce squares chocolate
1 cup flour, sifted
2 teaspoons baking powder
1/2 teaspoon baking soda
2/3 cup milk
1/2 cup chopped nuts
2/3 cup sugar
2 cups water
1/8 teaspoon salt

Serves 4 to 6

Preheat oven to 350 degrees. Cream shortening, salt, cinnamon, and sugar together and mix thoroughly. Melt 2 1-ounce squares of chocolate and blend in.

Mix together flour, baking powder, and baking soda. Add milk and chopped nuts. Blend both mixtures together to create batter.

Combine sugar, water, salt, and the remaining chocolate square in a pan and bring to a boil. Pour this hot mix into a greased baking dish. Drop the batter by spoonfuls on top of the syrup in the baking dish. Bake for 45 minutes.

Mrs. Shuster's Cheese Pie

Mike Shuster, **Correspondent**

My mother served this cheese pie at Thanksgiving and other family holidays. I think she got it out of a women's magazine way back in the 1950s. I get a good feeling about those times because I think of her when I make this pie. For a really great treat, make a sauce from fresh raspberries by forcing them through a sieve that catches the seeds. Drizzle it over each individual piece of pie.

PIE: Preheat oven to 325 degrees. Put the cream cheese in a bowl and beat in eggs, one at a time, until smooth. Add sugar and vanilla. Pour into a buttered pie pan (glass makes it look very nice).

Bake for 50 minutes or until golden brown. Pie will puff up, a little like a soufflé. Remove from oven and cool for 15 minutes. Pie will settle. Leave the oven on.

TOPPING: Mix together sour cream, sugar, and vanilla. After the pie has cooled for 15 minutes, pour topping onto the cooled pie, spreading evenly in the areas that have settled. Leave about 1/2-inch of pie edge visible above the topping.

Bake for 15 minutes more. Remove from oven. Let sit to cool. Chill in refrigerator. Serve cold.

Pie
2 8-ounce packages cream
    cheese, room temperature
3 eggs
2/3 cup sugar
1 teaspoon vanilla

Topping
1 pint sour cream
3 tablespoons sugar
1 teaspoon vanilla

Serves 4 to 6

Mrs. Walkinshaw's Dundee Cake

Fiona Ritchie, Host, *The Thistle & Shamrock*

The tale of this recipe comes from my story, "A Scottish Christmas Ceilidh," from the CD *A Thistle & Shamrock Christmas Ceilidh*. "Mrs. Walkinshaw was well known for her wonderful baking, and especially for her 'secret ingredient'... It was widely believed that the secret ingredient for all Mrs. Walkinshaw's baking was manufactured in a still in her back bedroom."

6 ounces butter or margarine
6 ounces superfine sugar
1 cup flour
1/2 teaspoon salt
1 teaspoon baking powder
1 teaspoon allspice
4 eggs
1 ounce ground almonds
4 ounces currants
8 ounces raisins
2 ounces candied peel
Scotch whisky, optional
1 ounce split, blanched almonds

Serves 4 to 6

Preheat oven to 325 degrees. Grease an 8-inch round cake pan and line with parchment paper. Cream the butter and sugar in a bowl. Sift the flour, salt, baking powder, and allspice together. Add the eggs and the flour mixture alternately to the creamed butter, beating well. Stir in the ground almonds, fruit, and peel. Gently mix. Add small dash of Scotch whisky, if desired.

Pour batter into the cake pan. Arrange the split almonds evenly on top of the cake. Bake for about 2 hours.

After the first hour if the top is browning too quickly, cover with parchment paper. Allow the cake to cool slightly in the pan before turning onto a wire rack. The cake will keep for several weeks if wrapped in kitchen foil.

Omi's Linzertorte

Jessica Goldstein, **Associate Producer**

This recipe comes from my *omi* (German for grandmother), who is from Freiberg, Germany. *Omi* — who is now 92 — left Germany in 1938, went to Brazil, and then later came to the U.S. Her recipe has survived all of her adventures. It is especially good when eaten a couple of days after it is baked.

Preheat oven to 350 degrees. Mix butter and sugar in a bowl until creamy. Add egg yolks and beat well. Stir in almonds, lemon rind and kirshwasser. Sift together flour, cinnamon, cloves, cocoa, and salt. Fold into the creamy mixture. Knead well and let rest in the refrigerator for 1 hour.

Pat 2/3 of dough into a 9-inch springform pan — it should be about 1/2-inch thick. Spread raspberry preserves on top of dough. Use the remaining dough to make strips for the latticework on top. Bake for 30 to 40 minutes until the top is slightly brown.

1/2 pound sweet butter
1 cup sugar
2 egg yolks
1-1/2 cups finely grated
    almonds
1-1/2 teaspoons grated lemon
    rind
1/2 teaspoon kirshwasser,
    optional
2 cups flour
2 teaspoons cinnamon
1/2 teaspoon grated cloves
1-1/2 teaspoons cocoa
1/2 teaspoon salt
Raspberry preserves

Serves 4 to 6

Oreo® Cheesecake

Barbara Bradley Hagerty, **Correspondent**

The only dish in my family that made repeat performances was my mom's corn pudding. Every Christmas, Thanksgiving, and Easter we could expect generous portions of the sweet yellow mash. Once the kids grew up and left the house, however, they avoided corn pudding at all costs, and the old family recipe was tucked away. So, instead of corn pudding, here's my offering for the best dessert on the planet, compliments of a chef friend of mine.

Crust
1 bag of Oreo® cookies
2 ounces butter, melted

Filling
32 ounces cream cheese
2 cups sugar
4 eggs
2 teaspoons vanilla extract

Serves 4 to 6

Preheat oven to 325 degrees. Using a food processor, crush the Oreo® cookies as finely as possible. Add melted butter and mix well. Set mixture aside.

Again using a food processor, mix cream cheese, sugar, eggs, and vanilla until smooth. Line an 8-inch springform pan with aluminum foil and lightly coat with butter. Firmly press the cookie mixture on the bottom of the pan, as evenly as possible. Spread the cream cheese filling over the crust.

Bake for 1 hour until the center becomes firm. Check for doneness by gently shaking the pan. Cook an additional 15 minutes if the center is still "runny." Remove from oven and cool. Chill for 2 hours. Serve with whipped cream and hot chocolate sauce.

Peg's Chewy One-pot Brownies

Peggy Girshman, **Assistant Managing Editor**

This is a simple recipe for brownies but one that has withstood the test of time and gets rapidly consumed. Then again, around NPR if you cooked a dead dog and put it out, it would be gone within a few hours.

Preheat oven to 375 degrees. Melt butter and chocolate in a saucepan. Remove from heat and cool a little. Add sugar and blend. Add eggs, one at a time, then add vanilla.

Stir in flour and baking powder. Add nuts, if you like nuts (My pal, Joanne Silberner, doesn't like nuts so I usually keep them out for her sake).

Bake in greased jellyroll pan for at least 25 minutes. Try not to overcook.

Cut into squares when cooled.

2 sticks butter (not margarine)
8 ounces bitter chocolate
4 cups sugar
6 eggs
1-1/2 tablespoons vanilla
2 cups flour
1-1/2 teaspoons baking powder
Nuts, if desired

Serves 6 to 8

Rhubarb Torte

Tom Gjelten, **Correspondent**

I've been a big rhubarb fan all my life. We used to have tons of it during the summer in Iowa, where I grew up. In my 20s, I lived on a farm on an island off the coast of Maine and to my great delight I found a huge rhubarb patch out behind the barn. I remembered this rhubarb dessert that my mother made that was just about my favorite thing of all. It's the only dessert I've actually made myself.

Preheat oven to 350 degrees. Mix flour, butter, and sugar to make crust. Spread it in a 9 x 9-inch pan. Pat it down. Bake 15 minutes.

Mix filling ingredients together and pour over crust. Bake 40 to 45 minutes.

Crust
1 cup flour
1/4 pound butter
5 tablespoons powdered sugar

Filling
2 eggs, beaten
1 1/2 cups sugar
1/4 teaspoon salt
1/2 teaspoon vanilla
3/4 teaspoon baking powder
1/4 cup flour
2 cups rhubarb, chopped

Serves 4 to 6

Scott's Apple Pie

Scott Horsley, **Reporter**

I made this pie for the first time when I was working for a radio station in New Hampshire. Apples are that state's number one cash crop, and I'd been working on a story about integrated pest management in the orchards outside Concord. I often make this pie for radio station potlucks (and even sold one for $40 in a recent public radio auction). Some tips: The crust is the big selling point. Mixing it by hand helps make it flaky. I use the same crust for cherry and berry pies, dusting the top with a little sugar instead of cinnamon. And it's important to slice the apples very thin so the filling gels.

Crust
2 cups flour
1 teaspoon salt
2/3 cup shortening
1/4 cup cold water

Filling
6 to 10 apples (about 5 cups)
1/2 cup sugar
Pinch salt
1/4 teaspoon cinnamon
1/8 teaspoon nutmeg
2 to 3 tablespoons flour (more or less, depending on how juicy the apples are)

Serves 6 to 8

CRUST: Sift flour and salt together, set aside 1/3 cup. Add shortening to the remaining dry mixture and mix with a fork until it forms small balls. Add cold water to the set-aside dry mix and stir. Combine both mixtures by hand. Divide and roll into two 9-inch crusts.

FILLING: Preheat oven to 450 degrees. Peel, core, and slice the apples thin. Add sugar, salt, cinnamon, nutmeg, and flour; mix by hand. Press one crust into 9-inch pie pan. Add filling. Cover with second crust and seal edges. Dot the top crust with 1 tablespoon of butter and, if desired, dust with cinnamon. Cut slits in top crust for steam. Bake for 10 minutes, reduce heat to 350 degrees and continue baking another 50 minutes.

Southern Buttermilk Pie

Andrea Danyo, **Publicity & Events Manager**

As the manager of the NPR speakers' bureau, I work with all the voices you hear to get them out speaking in your communities. To keep the on-air talent happy, I find this buttermilk pie does just the trick! Just like public radio, it's warm, rich, filling, and gets people talking.

Preheat oven to 350 degrees. Blend butter and sugar together until smooth and creamy. Add eggs, one at a time, until well blended. Add flour, vanilla, and nutmeg. Blend. Add the buttermilk (any kind except non-fat). Mix well. Pour mixture into frozen or homemade piecrust and bake for 45 minutes, until solid and lightly browned on top.

Serve warm with vanilla ice cream.

1 stick butter, softened
2 cups sugar
3 eggs
3 rounded tablespoons flour
1 teaspoon vanilla extract
Dash of nutmeg
1 cup buttermilk

Serves 4 to 6

Sugar Cookies to Die For

Korva Coleman, **Newscaster/Host**

It is an understatement to say I cannot cook. However, reliable sources tell me children fight over these cookies in the lunchroom when my kids take them to school. My children have tried to comfort me about my lack of culinary prowess so they wrote me a note that said, "Mom discovered she can't cook. So we decided to investigate. She couldn't cook meals but could make desserts. And boy can she cook! Her sugar cookies are great. So that qualifies her as a mom." I couldn't be more pleased.

1/4 pound butter
3/4 cup sugar
1 egg
1/2 teaspoon vanilla
1 tablespoon heavy cream
1-1/4 cups flour
1/4 teaspoon baking powder

Preheat the oven to 350 degrees. Cream the butter, and gradually add sugar until blended. Add the egg, vanilla, and cream. Pour in the flour and the baking powder and beat until thoroughly mixed. Put spoonfuls of the dough on an ungreased baking sheet and bake for 8 to 10 minutes, until light golden.

Note: You can substitute milk for the cream but it will never, ever, ever taste as good.

Index

NPR: Our Secret Recipe

In kitchens and culinary schools, diners and dining rooms, more than 22 million people each week consume heaping helpings of NPR's diverse menu of award-winning news, talk, music, and entertainment programming. They savor the sound of NPR, which has set the standard for flavorful storytelling. Together with our member stations, NPR satisfies your hunger for intellectually nutritious and culturally delicious radio.

The secret ingredients in this renowned recipe? Award-winning programming from NPR, your local station's strong commitment to public service, and you!

Combine all ingredients. Mix until well blended. Add a heaping helping of humor to taste.

Mix well, and enjoy often!

32 award-winning programs
(Over 100 hours worth)
778 NPR stations nationwide
Hundreds of incredibly talented
reporters, producers, editors,
directors, and more
Your radio
You

Serves Millions